CRYPTOCUR INVESTING GUIDE FOR BEGINNERS

Learn the Basics of How to Buy and Sell Bitcoins and Many More Crypto Currencies, Blockchains, and Cryptography

Shawn Colon

© Copyright 2022 by SHZ Publications. All right reserved.

All right reserved. This work is meant to provide relevant information on the topic described in the title only for knowledge purposes. The author has tried to provide accurate and factual information, but no claim can be made as to their accuracy or validity since the author has not claimed to be an expert.

Throughout the United States, the American Bar Association and the Committee of Publishers Association consider this statement legally binding. Other jurisdictions can implement their own laws. Any reproduction, transmission, or copying of any of the materials contained within the work without the express written consent of the copyright holder will be considered a violation. Any additional work derived from this material will be the property of the copyright holder.

The data, dates, events, descriptions, and all other information contained within the work are assumed to be true, fair, and accurate unless the work has been specifically described as one of fiction. Publishers are not responsible for the actions taken by readers in connection with these works, regardless of their nature. The publisher acknowledges that the reader acts on their own accord and that no responsibility can be taken by the author or Publisher for the reader's observance of the tips, advice, counsel, strategies, and techniques that may be provided in this book.

Dear readers

Welcome to the Cryptocurrency investing guide for beginners; I am a US-based writer who is passionate about helping beginners make a living from their artistic talent. I firmly believe in the principles of Philosophy and that people should live their dreams and not get sucked into a life of doing something they don't like.

As a teacher, investor, gamer, and avid coffee nerd who loves to meditate and keep things sane in this overthinking world, I welcome you all into this beautiful journey with open arms. I thank you for taking the first step into this exciting crypto world.

The Crypto world is filled with vast money-making opportunities and complex technical terms, which one needs to understand to avail of all these fruitful opportunities. In this book, I have attempted my best to explain these complexities in the simplest terms, allowing even a beginner to understand them.

Please keep in mind that it will all make sense as you proceed through the chapters, as everything is explained in their respective chapters. I recommend going slow through chapters, and reading twice will help you a lot to understand these terms and their functions.

I hope you enjoy the book! Happy reading!

Please leave an honest review on amazon; it will only take 3 mins of yours, but it makes a big difference to me. A positive review from wonderful customers like you help other readers feel confident about choosing the Cryptocurrency investing guide for beginners. Sharing your happy experience will be greatly appreciated!

If you want to learn more in-depth knowledge about NFTs and explore them to the fullest, you can get all the details about how to create, buy and sell NFTs in my other book - **NFT Beginners Handbook: Create, Buy and Sell Non-Fungible Tokens with Ease** by Shawn Colon.

To receive a digital copy for free, please enroll in our reader's email list:

Please visit:

https://shzpublication.systeme.io/8c42dbdb

Table of Contents

CRYPTOCURRENCY INVESTING GUIDE FOR BEGINNERS _____ 1

INTRODUCTION _____ 10
- WHAT IS CRYPTOCURRENCY? _____ 11
- WHAT IS BLOCKCHAIN TECHNOLOGY? _____ 13
- WHO IS SATOSHI NAKAMOTO, AND WHY WAS CRYPTO REQUIRED? _ 15
- STATE OF THE CURRENT MARKET IN 2022 _____ 16
- THE EVOLUTION OF MONEY AND THE FUTURE OF CRYPTOCURRENCIES _____ 17

CHAPTER 1: CRYPTOCURRENCY _____ 19

DETAILED ANALYSIS OF CRYPTOCURRENCY _____ 20
- HOW DOES CRYPTOCURRENCY WORK? _____ 22
- DIFFERENT TYPES OF CRYPTO CURRENCIES _____ 23
- WHAT ARE STABLECOINS? _____ 25
- WHAT IS CRYPTOPIA? _____ 28
- WHAT ARE BITCOINS? _____ 28
- WHY ARE BITCOINS THE HOTTEST TOPIC IN THE CRYPTO WORLD? _ 30
- WHAT IS THE POINT OF CRYPTO CURRENCY? _____ 31

CHAPTER 2: BLOCKCHAINS _____ 34
- WHAT IS A BLOCKCHAIN? _____ 34
- COMMON BLOCKCHAIN TECHNOLOGIES _____ 36
- SIMPLE BLOCKCHAIN EXAMPLES _____ 38
- PUBLIC BLOCKCHAINS _____ 41
- HOW TO REVIEW BLOCKCHAIN ARCHITECTURE? _____ 43
- MERITS OF BLOCKCHAINS _____ 43

DRAWBACKS OF BLOCKCHAINS _____ 46
WHAT IS CRYPTOGRAPHY? _____ 47

CHAPTER 3: WALLETS _____ 49

WHAT IS A DIGITAL WALLET? _____ 49
WHY IS WALLET IMPORTANT? _____ 53
HOW TO SAFELY STORE YOUR COINS IN YOUR WALLET? _____ 54
HOW TO SECURE YOUR WALLET FROM HACKERS? _____ 57
WHAT ARE THE BEST PLATFORMS TO BUY AND SELL CRYPTOCURRENCY?
_____ 59

CHAPTER 4: RISK MANAGEMENT _____ 62

WHAT ARE THE DIFFERENT KINDS OF RISK? _____ 62
HOW CAN YOU MEASURE THESE RISKS? _____ 69
HOW TO MANAGE THE RISKS AND AVOID THEM? _____ 71
HOW TO WATCH OUT FOR THE IMPORTANT THINGS WHILE TRADING IN CRYPTO? _____ 73

CHAPTER 5: PORTFOLIO ANALYSIS _____ 75

HOW CAN YOU BUILD A CRYPTO PORTFOLIO? _____ 76
WHAT DO YOU MEAN BY ASSET ALLOCATION? _____ 79
WHAT IS PORTFOLIO REBALANCING? _____ 80
HOW TO REBALANCE YOUR PORTFOLIO? _____ 84
WHAT IS FUNDAMENTAL ANALYSIS OF CRYPTOCURRENCY MARKETS? 87

CHAPTER 6: HOW TO INVEST IN CRYPTOCURRENCIES? _____ 90

HOW TO FIND AND CHOOSE BETWEEN TOP CRYPTOCURRENCIES IN THE MARKET? _____ 90
WHAT STRATEGIES CAN YOU FOLLOW FOR CRYPTO TRADING? ____ 94
HOW TO DETERMINE THE VALUE OF CRYPTOCURRENCY? _____ 97
WHICH ARE THE BEST PLATFORMS FOR TRADING CRYPTOCURRENCY?
_____ 100

What Do You Understand by Value Investing? _____ 102

CHAPTER 7: HOW TO TRADE CRYPTOCURRENCY? _____ 104

How Is Blockchain Used? _____ 104
Trading Cryptocurrency _____ 105
How to Do a Technical Analysis to Find Out What Are the Best Margins, Options, and Future? _____ 106
Cryptocurrency Trading Strategy _____ 106
How to Avoid Common Mistakes That Most Traders Make 108
Supply and Demand _____ 112
How to Evaluate Crypto Technologies? _____ 114

CHAPTER 8: DIGITAL TOKENS _____ 116

What Are Digital Tokens? _____ 116
How Are Digital Tokens Useful? _____ 117
Difference Between Digital Tokens and Coins _____ 118
Token Sales _____ 121
Types of Token Sales _____ 122
Where to Find These Types of Offerings and What to Keep In Mind While Researching Them _____ 124
Decentralized Finance (DeFi) _____ 125
DeFi Platforms and How to Use Them _____ 127
Borrowing and Lending of DeFi _____ 128

CHAPTER 9: MINING _____ 130

What Is Mining? _____ 130
How Does Mining Work? _____ 131
How Can One Mine Cryptocurrency? _____ 132
What Is Staking? _____ 135
How Is Staking Done? _____ 135
Crypto Mining Rigs and Electricity _____ 138
Best Mining Platforms _____ 139

- Risks of Mining and Staking — 142
- Rewards of Mining and Staking — 142

CHAPTER 10: NFT — 144
- Different Types of NFT and How It Works — 145
- What Are High-Value NFTs? — 147
- How to Buy and Sell NFT — 148
- Best Platforms for NFT — 149
- Risk Regarding NFT — 152

CONCLUSION — 156

ABOUT THE AUTHOR — 164

INTRODUCTION

In the years that have gone by, technology has advanced significantly with the introduction of cryptocurrency and blockchains. Although these terms may sound intriguing to the ear, their actual meaning can sometimes be overlooked or misunderstood. Suppose you have limited knowledge of digital technology but would like to know more about cryptocurrencies or blockchain technology and how it has shaped the digital world. In that case, this book may serve as your go-to solution.

Digital technology and assets may feel too complex to understand. Still, by breaking their core elements into easy-to-understand definitions and explaining their mechanisms, you may quickly develop an interest in cryptocurrencies and the Blockchain. With the help of this book, you can further your knowledge about these topics, thus helping you make an informed decision about whether to begin your crypto journey.

WHAT IS CRYPTOCURRENCY?

Firstly, you should understand what a cryptocurrency is and what it stands for. In the same way that dollars are used as the currency in the US, we use a currency called "Cryptocurrency" or "Crypto" in the digital world. This digital currency is backed by cryptography, making it next to impossible for anyone to counterfeit it. Cryptocurrency is a tradable asset and is built on blockchain technology. Bitcoin, which you may have heard of, was the world's first cryptocurrency. Since then, there have been numerous additions to the list, and as of now, there are over 15,000 cryptocurrencies in the digital world.

In general, cryptocurrencies can be divided into four types based on their utility. These are:

- **Asset** - These types of cryptocurrencies have the value of an external asset(Investments, properties, or commodities). They act as a tokenized version of an asset that can be embedded into a blockchain for easy transaction and value exchange. Examples of Asset types are Stablecoins such as Tether (USDT), Binance USD (BUSD), Digix Gold token (DGX), and more.

- **Meme or Joke Coins** - The digital world is incomplete without an element of fun and excitement. Originally created for entertainment, meme coins were made, which act as a type of crypto nowadays. You may have heard or read about Dogecoins (featuring an image of a Shiba Inu Dog). Dogecoins started their journey as meme coins and soon became one of the highly talked about cryptocurrencies in the digital world. Other such meme coins include Dogelon Mars (ELON) and Shiba Inu (SHIB).

- **Financing for Projects -** Cryptocurrencies of this type were designed to be used in financing special projects that would aim to solve problems in the world. For example, Decentraland was created, an Ethereum-based application that allows users to buy virtual land using MANA, the application's cryptocurrency. Another example would be Siacoin (SIA), which aims to solve the problem of expensive cloud storage.

- **Cross-Border Transactions-** The purpose of this type of crypto was to make cross-border payment transactions quicker and cheaper. Cross-border payments are those in which the recipient or the sender resides in a different country. With time the values of these cryptocurrencies have increased magnificently. An example of this type of cryptocurrency is the very famous Bitcoin.

WHAT IS BLOCKCHAIN TECHNOLOGY?

Blockchain technology organizes and monitors cryptocurrency, thus acting as a peer-to-peer network, so it is crucial to understand what blockchain technology does. Blockchain can be described as a decentralized system of information storage that makes it impossible to hack into or cheat. More simply, it can be understood as a network of computers (nodes) sharing the same information about all the transactions made. In other words, instead of storing all the transaction history in a single computer, the transaction history is distributed throughout the entire worldwide network of computers and is stored in multiple locations.

Blockchain technology allows the existence of cryptocurrencies and it has many benefits. A few of these benefits include:

- **Decentralized Structure** - In other words, Blockchain enables a shared ecosystem of data to be shared through a common platform, which reduces chaos and dilemma and helps build trust and transparency.

- **High Speed** - Compared to a traditional method of handling transactions, the blockchain takes considerably less time and is significantly faster than other methods. It is notable that even with heavy traffic, the speed of completing transactions remains high and beats that of different technologies.

- **Immutability** - Whenever a transaction is made on a blockchain, it is permanently recorded and cannot be altered or deleted after its completion. All the recorded transactions have the date and time on them, so there is rarely a chance of duplicating or altering, thereby making them reliable and secured.

- **Tokenization** - Using blockchain technology, assets, whether they be digital or physical, can be tokenized and converted into digital tokens. These can then be shared on a blockchain platform, where they can be easily transferable between the users. These tokens can be digital artworks or other assets, which make business transactions much more straightforward and hassle-free.

WHO IS SATOSHI NAKAMOTO, AND WHY WAS CRYPTO REQUIRED?

Satoshi Nakamoto is a fictitious name used by the person or group of people who came up with Bitcoin and penned the original Bitcoin whitepaper. Until 2010, Satoshi Nakamoto was active online and would discuss the development of Bitcoin and came up with the workings related to it, called Bitcoin "whitepaper" in 2008. It has now been a little over a decade since Satoshi Nakamoto has been inactive online and only shows up occasionally. Many people around the world, amateurs as well as computer experts, have tried to unmask the identity of Satoshi Nakamoto but have yet to come to a definite conclusion. Satoshi Nakamoto remains a mystery; their identity has not been discovered.

A cryptocurrency called bitcoin was first used as a currency in 2009 and was intended to act as a peer-to-peer cash system that could be used similarly to a bank account. But it gradually became the prime interest of investors who were keen on cryptocurrencies. They started collecting and trading them, which quickly increased the currency's value. In February 2011, one Bitcoin (BTC) was worth $1, and as of now, when writing this book, it is priced at approximately $43,000.

Cryptocurrencies became popular very quickly as they could be bought digitally without difficulty, and there were a lot of currencies to choose from. The exchange of currencies was also not a problem due to the presence of a feature called e-wallet or crypto-wallet, with the help of which users could easily exchange currencies with a minimum transaction fee. With cryptocurrency, the transaction cost is minimal for transferring money from a digital wallet to a bank account compared to other fiat currency methods.

STATE OF THE CURRENT MARKET IN 2022

As of 2022, the cryptocurrency market is valued at over $2.2 trillion. In the year 2021 alone, the crypto market saw an increase of 187.5% from the previous year, when it was worth $1.49 billion. It is estimated that the crypto market has experienced a growth of 21% since the beginning of 2022. According to crypto-enthusiasts, few cryptocurrencies may stand out and make it big. Some of these are Bitcoin, Dogecoin, Lucky Block, Ether, and Binance Coin. Although one may not know for sure which of these will make it to the top spot, one can only make a guess and wait to see if they prevail.

THE EVOLUTION OF MONEY AND THE FUTURE OF CRYPTOCURRENCIES

With the evolution of money from being made of paper and traded hand to hand or, more recently, electronically transferred and stored in digital wallets, one can only ponder and marvel. Even up to three decades earlier, one could only imagine such a reality where physical assets could be sold on the internet using digital currency and traded on blockchain technology. Still, today it has become a reality accepted by all. Just like every new development that changes the world, cryptocurrencies have left an imprint on digital technology forever.

The world of cryptocurrencies has steadily continued to gather a tremendous amount of attention since the year they were first introduced and has shown massive growth in value over the decades. One can go as far as to say that they may very well be here for a good long while and see progressive growth in the years to come, due to a few reasons, such as:

- **Investment Option** - So far, the world of crypto has managed to provide us with everything we could expect. As time goes on, experts say that the market will accommodate changes to improve the platform and incorporate more options that will bring long time benefits and prove to be a rewarding investment option.

- **Powerful Financial Technology** - Trading with cryptocurrencies is way faster than other fiat currency methods. It has been consistently evolving and challenging our money concepts and how we manage them. So far, our achievements are just stepping stones and building blocks to a more incredible, dynamic, and financial growth structure.

- **Gaining Popularity** - There are more and more people who accept and have publicly acknowledged cryptocurrencies as part of their daily finance and have publicly acknowledged them. It also includes people of high social status, such as actors, financial advisors, investors, and technology-focused corporations. With publicity, more and more people have shown interest in cryptocurrencies and joined in the journey.

Whether the hype will continue to grow over the next few decades or not, one has to wait to see it. Still, one thing is for sure: cryptocurrency will never be entirely gone from digital technology. I am certain it will stay here for a few more decades.

CHAPTER 1: CRYPTOCURRENCY

Let's see how cryptocurrency came into existence; it's time to dive into details. Learning the basics is an excellent way to start. Still, one must continue beyond basics to achieve sufficient and accurate knowledge in a particular field. And to accomplish that and learn more about this field of digital technology, you must keep moving forward and dive deeper into the world of crypto. The more you progress through these chapters, the more you will diversify your understanding and knowledge about it.

In this chapter, you will find yourself diving into the inner specifics of cryptocurrency, how it functions, the different types of currencies that are available for public use, and their purposes. You will also learn about the most hyped cryptocurrency-"Bitcoin," and why it is such a hot topic. Overall, this chapter will give you an intermediate level of knowledge and understanding of the crypto world and the constituents that make it up.

DETAILED ANALYSIS OF CRYPTOCURRENCY

Cryptocurrency is a digital currency that allows users to trade assets (digital or physical) on blockchain technology. Which generally uses cryptography as its main element. But what does cryptography mean? Cryptography, also called cryptology, involves generating and creating codes that allow specific information to remain confidential. Using cryptography, it is possible to convert the data into an encrypted format so unauthorized users cannot read it. In this way, it ensures that an unauthorized party cannot compromise data during data transfer. The data is "encrypted" in such a format that no one can read the information on it without a "decryption key."

Cryptocurrency is becoming a popular method for trading goods and services online. They are also not issued by a central authority, unlike traditional fiat money. When a person carries out a transaction using cryptocurrencies, it gets recorded in a public ledger. Cryptocurrency exists only in the online/digital world as it does not have a physical form or shape. Online exchanges are used as a medium for transferring cryptocurrencies from one user to another.
With the introduction of cryptocurrency, the digital world gained new heights. However, it is still a

controversial topic among people, particularly among the youth. While some consider it an advancement, some critics consider it an abomination. Economists like Warren Buffet and Paul Krugman have called Bitcoin a "mirage" and "evil." At the same time, venture capitalist Marc Andreessen believes cryptocurrency is "the next internet." The world of crypto has left the world divided. Still, most of the people who have invested in it do not seem to have any animosity toward it but instead seem to be enjoying the journey.

HOW DOES CRYPTOCURRENCY WORK?

Cryptocurrency units are generated by a process called mining, which requires powerful software and hardware. During mining, two things happen:

1. **Verification of Cryptocurrency Transactions-** A single computer is not powerful enough to successfully and profitably carry out verification of cryptocurrency transactions, as doing so requires a massive amount of electricity and power. Hence, this solution involves miners (different computer users) joining pools to create a considerable computing power that can facilitate the verification process.

2. **Creation of New Units of Cryptocurrency-** After the miners successfully achieve enough power to start the verification, the blockchain allocates mining profits to the participants as a reward for verifying the transactions. There is competition among miners as to who can complete the verification process of all the pending transactions, thereby reaping the most profit from it. The leveraging of specialized hardware and the accumulation of cheaper electricity makes the miners want to maximize their profits and compete against one another, which further ensures the integrity of transactions.

The majority of mining pools are located in China and make up over 70% of the total Bitcoin mining. Some of the largest mining pools are AntPool, which makes up about 19% of the total mining pools, followed by BTC.TOP constitutes 11.6%, and BTC.com makes up 10%. Other mining pools include F2Pool (8.9%), Bixin (8.6%), BTCC Pool (7.2%), BitFurry (5.6%), and many more.

DIFFERENT TYPES OF CRYPTO CURRENCIES

In this subheading, I will elaborate on the types of cryptocurrencies that a person can choose from and what makes them unique from the rest. Almost all types of cryptocurrencies being used today are derived in some way or the other from Bitcoin. Following are some of the most famous cryptocurrencies and the functions they perform.

1.   **Ethereum (ETH)** - "Ethereum" is a blockchain-based currency which is also known as "Ether." They have gained popularity over the years and are one of the most frequently used cryptocurrencies. Ethereum works on a decentralized platform. It ensures that participants can create and use smart contracts and decentralized applications or dApps without interference from third parties,

control, or fraud. It was launched in 2015 and quickly became the second-largest currency used in the digital network.

2.   **Altcoin** - These are the cryptocurrencies modeled after Bitcoin, although it lacks the amount of security provided by Bitcoin. The altcoin has certain features different from Bitcoin, including having the power to handle more transactions per second and using proof of stake and other such consensus algorithms.

3.   **Tether (USDT)** - This type of cryptocurrency was one the earliest and is extremely popular in a group called stablecoins. It was launched in 2014 and allowed users to use the blockchain network and other technologies during the transaction using traditional currencies. It dramatically reduces the complexity and volatility often carried by digital currencies. It has so far made a market cap of $80.1 billion.

4.   **Dogecoin (DOGE)** - This type of cryptocurrency was created as a joke and was a "meme coin." It was built in 2013 by Billy Markus and Jackson Palmer, a pair of software engineers. It was intended to be purely for entertainment purposes. But, it soon became much more popular than expected, and its price skyrocketed by 2021. As of 2022, Dogecoin's market capitalization is slightly over $15 billion, whereas one DOGE is priced at

almost 11 cents. It stands today as the 13th largest cryptocurrency in the digital world.

5. **Binance Coin (BNB)** - Binance was previously used on the Ethereum blockchain as an ERC-20 token. This platform is also decentralized and functions as a method of payment when trading on Binance Exchange. If we look at market capitalization, it has become the third-largest cryptocurrency in the market. One reason for this could be that users can avail themselves of discounts if they use the Binance token as a means of payment. As of 2022, the market capitalization of Binance Coin is a little over $61 billion.

Apart from the ones mentioned here, there are other cryptocurrencies used, such as Monero (XMR), Stellar (XLM), Polkadot (DOT), Cardano (ADA), Litecoin (LTC), and many more.

WHAT ARE STABLECOINS?

Stablecoins, as the name suggests, are a type of cryptocurrency, specifically Ethereum (ETH) tokens, which have their value associated with an external asset, such as gold or the US dollar, to stabilize its value. It means that even if the value of ETH changes, the value of Stablecoins remains the same. The purpose that Stablecoins serve is added stability compared to other cryptocurrencies, whose values occasionally alter. While the value of cryptocurrencies is mainly dependent on the market, Stablecoins are designed in such a way that their values tend to remain steady most of the time.

There are different types of Stablecoins that you can purchase, depending upon what is most convenient for you. They are:

- **Fiat-Backed Stablecoins**- These involve using traditional currencies such as dollars or other conventional fiat currencies in your bank account. You can use the fiat currency to purchase fiat Stablecoins, which you can redeem later for your original currency. These types of Stablecoins tend to be the ones with the least fluctuations in value.

- **Precious Metal-Backed Stablecoins**- You can also use metals with high market value to purchase Stablecoins, such as Gold. An example of these stablecoin backed by Gold would be Digix. These types of stablecoins are centralized but are protected from the volatility that cryptocurrencies generally have.

- **Crypto-Backed Stablecoins**- These stablecoins are backed by crypto assets and are over-collateralized, i.e., the value of the cryptocurrency held in reserves exceeds the value of the issued stablecoin to ensure its value. These stablecoins are less stable than fiat-backed stablecoins as they are highly volatile. DAI, which runs on the Ethereum blockchain, is an excellent example of the stablecoin crypto.

- **Algorithmic Stablecoins-** These stablecoins are unique because they use a computer algorithm to stop the coin's value from changing so much. For instance, if the value of such stablecoin rises, the algorithm automatically generates and dispatches more tokens into the platform to lower the value of the stablecoin, thereby maintaining its original price. An example of algorithmic stablecoin is Frax and AMPL.

WHAT IS CRYPTOPIA?

Cryptopia was founded in 2014 by Adam Clark and Rob Dawson and is a platform for cryptocurrency exchange. It is based in New Zealand. Many users and traders have reviewed the software so far as an enthusiastic technology for business people and loved it for its arbitrage features and extensive knowledge base. Most people using cryptopia have positive things to say about the software. It has been said to have a good standard business market interface, an extensive collection of coins, and quick response scripts.

Crytopia, is a novel approached and has faced its share of challenges and problems. In 2019, Cryptopia suffered a breach in security which resulted in a loss of almost 16 million worth of Ether and ERC-20 tokens. After Cryptopia went into liquidation in the same year, Russell Moore and David Ruscoe from New Zealand were appointed liquidators.

WHAT ARE BITCOINS?

Bitcoin is one of the most popular cryptocurrencies on the market. It was created in 2009 under Satoshi Nakamoto, a pseudonym, as you have already learned in the previous chapter. The technology behind Bitcoin may be complicated, but making payments or transactions using Bitcoin is pretty simple and uses a smartphone or digital wallet. This is a requirement that both the sender and the receiver must meet. Currently, even Microsoft accepts payments via Bitcoin as of today. If you think that that is not already exciting enough, you would be surprised to know that Subway has also started to accept Bitcoin payments as well!

Bitcoin definitely has its own set of benefits, seeing that it is a type of cryptocurrency. But there are a few things about Bitcoin that you should know before indulging in them. Bitcoin is known for only allowing seven transactions in a second. Some other cryptocurrencies are known to carry out more transactions in a second; Bitcoin can lag slightly in this case. Another minor inconvenience experienced by users is that the amount of time it takes to perform a transaction using Bitcoin is longer than it would take to do the same thing using some other types of cryptocurrencies.

Sharing or transferring bitcoins is very easy. It's just like you send a computer document from your PC to another via a sharing media or device; similarly, people can send Bitcoins to one another via digital wallets. This is backed in such a way that every transaction made is recorded in the Blockchain. This makes tracing a Bitcoin transaction easy and prevents unauthorized users from replicating or fabricating transactions.

WHY ARE BITCOINS THE HOTTEST TOPIC IN THE CRYPTO WORLD?

Bitcoins have gained a significant increase in popularity since the very famous Elon Musk posted his thoughts on his social media, saying it was a "good thing." Since then, his comment gained Bitcoin more and more buyers, which resulted in a rise in its value. The market cap of Bitcoin is over 778.42 billion. Elon Musk further showed his support for Bitcoin by changing his Twitter bio to "#Bitcoin," which surprised the world.

In January 2021, in an online chat with social media users, he also accepted that he was a huge supporter of Bitcoin. This endorsement further increased the sales of Bitcoin and made it one of the most talked-about cryptocurrencies in the digital world. It is not every day that the wealthiest man in the world publicly announces his support for a particular cryptocurrency with such devotion.

While it may be difficult to pinpoint the exact reason for the massive popularity of Bitcoins over the past decade, one can only make guesses. One of the reasons could be that since transactions using Bitcoins have no connections with the bank or government, people are keen to try it out and experience something new. This also allows people to spend their Bitcoins without anyone keeping track of their expenses and reasonably anonymously. It might have attracted the attention of people as well. Even if the records of all transactions are stored in public access, no one would be able to know what transactions you have made unless they know your account number, which is highly confidential.

WHAT IS THE POINT OF CRYPTO CURRENCY?

Cryptocurrency has garnered massive fame in a brief period, and this often leaves people wondering what the point of this is all about. Well, cryptocurrencies have become a household name because they have brought a new twist to the digital world and served multiple purposes. Some of the benefits of cryptocurrencies are detailed below:

- **Reduced Transaction Cost -** One of the most significant benefits of using crypto is that it eliminates the need for mediators from the transactions, automatically reducing the transaction costs and making it relatively much cheaper than other financial services.

- **High Transaction Speed -** Another important benefit of using cryptocurrency is the high speed of transactions. In a world where most transactions at US financial institutions take up to 3-5 days, cryptocurrency transactions can be completed within a matter of seconds or, at most, minutes.

- **Privacy Offered** - Trading in cryptocurrency offers users a higher level of privacy as one is not required to register for an account at any financial institution to be able to make a transaction in crypto. All you need to do is have a crypto-wallet, which is safe to use and does not compromise your personal information, and then you are good to go.

- **Easy Access** - There is no age limitation for individuals to trade crypto as long as they have a smartphone or computer and access to the internet. Setting up a crypto-wallet is also very quick compared to traditional financial systems.

- **High Security** - All your transactions require you to have a private key that helps you gain access to your digital wallet. This makes signing into someone else's wallet very difficult, as, without the specific key, you cannot do so. Another factor that makes crypto transactions so secure is that it requires a massive amount of computer power to place an attack on the blockchain network. In addition, modifying the blockchain network is very expensive.

Placing all these benefits together gives us an idea as to why cryptocurrencies are gradually becoming increasingly popular and are being adopted by more and more institutions and facilities.

CHAPTER 2: BLOCKCHAINS

Meet the new buzzword in town – Blockchain! It is the futuristic database technology that forms the core behind all cryptocurrencies. It stores information in a digitally distributed database that is shared across all the users in a network. Since identical replicas of the database are copied and spread across the network, it becomes extremely difficult for fraudsters to cheat or hack the system. Blockchains help maintains a secure and trusted decentralized platform for performing transactions based on cryptocurrencies.

WHAT IS A BLOCKCHAIN?

Blockchain is an immutable, shared ledger that helps track and record transactions across a digital network. No matter what type of asset you have, Blockchain can be used to keep records of each and everything. Be it tangible assets like your house, car, or land that you can touch or intangible assets such as patents, copyrights, or branding rights that you cannot touch with your hand. Blockchains offer an ideal solution for all crypto-based transactions, purchasing of NFTs, and smart DeFi contracts because of their robust and multi-purpose nature.

What's so unique about Blockchain that makes it so popular? Indeed the information stored in the Blockchain can also be stored in any conventional database. Then, what sets Blockchain apart from the rest? The answer is very simple. Blockchain's uniqueness lies in the fact that it is entirely decentralized. None of your transaction details or asset information lies in one single server or is managed by a central authority. Blockchain uses data replication to ensure protection and reliability.

So, how does Blockchain work? The name itself implies that it's a chain of individual data blocks that keeps increasing as and when new data gets added periodically. All other nodes update their copy of the blockchain ledger to remain legit. Creating new data blocks is highly secure information. However, when any new data block has to be created, it must be verified by most of the existing nodes before it gets added to the ledger. It makes Blockchain stand out from the conventional standalone databases, where people can make changes without consulting others. Once the block has been verified, its transactions are updated in the ledger and distributed among all the users.

COMMON BLOCKCHAIN TECHNOLOGIES

Blockchain technology, created as the foundation for cryptocurrency, has evolved and spread across many more applications over the years. Various sectors have been revolutionized by it, and a new future has emerged.

Ethereum

Ethereum is a well-known blockchain platform that provides a variety of features for its users. It is one of the earliest blockchain platforms and has a vibrant community of researchers and developers. Many organizations prefer Ethereum because of its cost-effectiveness and easy scalability. Its decentralized nature also gives scope for creativity and innovation required in the business industry.

Tron

Looking for an operating system based on Blockchain? Tron is your answer. It has thus become the world's fastest-growing blockchain network because of its growing user base. Tron offers greater freedom to content creators who wish to showcase their talent. The scalability of Tron and its multi-language extension are also notable features.

IBM Blockchain

Those in the IT field are sure to be familiar with IBM. With the company's own Blockchain, you can create and grow a blockchain network and create an environment that fits the way you want it to be by simply configuring it. If you're thinking that building such a blockchain network is lengthy and complicated, IBM's group of experts is there to help you. IBM blockchain is well known for its transparency and accessible configuration facilities.

SIMPLE BLOCKCHAIN EXAMPLES

In order to understand Bitcoin, you have to know that blockchains store information about monetary transactions. Similarly, there are thousands of other cryptocurrency networks running on a blockchain. Sounds powerful, right? Blockchain is essentially a reliable and secure method of storing information and other transactional data. Big companies like Siemens, Pfizer, IBM, Walmart, and many more have implemented blockchain technology in their operational model.

Why have blockchains become so popular? Why are people finding blockchains so reliable? Blockchain makes it possible for brands to get a complete picture of their products, from their source to their final destination, including all the stops and exchanges they went through before getting successfully delivered. All types of products, whether they're virtual or physical, fall under this category. Thus the companies can now check everything that the product came in contact with, making the fault identification process easier and faster. Here are some areas where blockchains are being utilized in order to better understand their efficiency.

Banking

The banking sector will be the first thing that comes to mind when we consider incorporating blockchains. Generally, banks are open five days a week and accept transactions only during business hours. Due to this, you cannot deposit checks during the weekends and must wait until the bank resumes operations on Monday. Moreover, even if you deposit within working hours, the transaction will likely take two or three days to get verified and issued because of the high volume of daily transactions the banks have to handle.

Blockchains are always running without having a single day off! By incorporating blockchain technology into financial transactions, customers can have their dealings verified and completed within 10-15 minutes, even on holiday. As well as helping banks exchange funds between various institutions safely and securely, blockchains have also been used in stock and money markets to facilitate the exchange of funds.

Cryptocurrency

What can be the best example of blockchains, if not crypto? They are the foundation of all cryptocurrencies, such as Bitcoin, Ethereum, and many others. Why are many people acclaiming crypto to be the future? If you look at the national currency system that is in place in all the countries around the world, you will find that a central authority is regulating it. Your currency and data are, therefore, vulnerable to the whims and fancies of the bank. Moreover, what will happen if the bank where you have your account falls into bankruptcy or the government at the place is very unstable? You will only run the risk of losing all your money!

Blockchains bring in the concept of decentralization. By involving multiple networks of computers, they allow cryptocurrencies to operate without any central governing body. It effectively reduces the chances of risk and also removes the need for any transactional and processing fees that the banks usually take. You can still make transactions or do business at the domestic and international level while living in a country with an unstable economy with the help of cryptocurrencies and blockchains.

Real Estate

Have you ever spent time at the local recorder's office? If so, you may know how tedious and inefficient the whole process is! If you have bought a property recently, a physical deed must be delivered to the government at the regional recording office so that the document may be manually added to the country's central database and public index. Whenever there is a property dispute or a compensation claim, the public index is revisited to determine if a resolution can be reached.

Don't you think the process is too time-consuming, expensive, and error-prone? A single erroneous entry can cost you the ownership of your property. Why not opt for the better?

Blockchains eliminate the need to scan and track deeds in the local recording office. People can stay assured that their property rights are safely recorded in the blockchain network. Once created, they cannot be falsely claimed by someone else because of the unique identification number associated with each transaction entry in the chain

PUBLIC BLOCKCHAINS

Permissioned blockchains can be acquired, and permissionless blockchains can be created, or a combination of both. In permissionless blockchains, any random user, including you, can pseudo-anonymously become a participating member of the network. In contrast, permissioned blockchains restrict access to the network to certain specific nodes along with their functionalities. Permissionless blockchains are considered more secure than permissioned blockchains because of the massive amount of nodes required for validating a piece of information, thereby helping the network prune out bad nodes. However, permissionless blockchains also suffer from the problem of larger transaction processing time because of the large number of nodes involved in the process.

Public blockchains are permissionless in nature and allow every node to participate in the network equally. They are the perfect examples of a decentralized network. Therefore, any node can read, write, or verify the data present in the Blockchain. Since any single authority does not control the data, it is difficult to alter the existing transactions that have been logged in the public Blockchain. The most well-known examples of a public blockchain are Bitcoin, Litecoin, and Ethereum. On such public blockchains, each individual node can mine cryptocurrencies by creating blocks for the requested transactions through the process of solving cryptographic equations. These miners are rewarded with a small amount of cryptocurrency for their hard work.

Public blockchains might suffer from certain drawbacks, such as reduced privacy of the transactions, as the ledger contents are visible to every participating member of the network. Therefore, a hybrid blockchain can be used. A single authority controls this blockchain, but certain transaction verification processes are carried out like a public blockchain; it's a mix of both worlds.

HOW TO REVIEW BLOCKCHAIN ARCHITECTURE?

Blockchains are a decentralized way of recording transactions that offer many benefits, and their potential keeps growing. As blockchains have enhanced the user's privacy and have strict security measures in place, it is clear that they will find their application in many other fields besides those mentioned above. However, like everything else, blockchains also suffer from little drawbacks. Let's look at both the merits and demerits of blockchains :

MERITS OF BLOCKCHAINS

- **Data Accuracy** – A Blockchain-based transaction requires the approval of several hundreds of computers. This eliminates the involvement of any humans in the process, thereby reducing the scope of human errors and increasing the accuracy of the stored information. Moreover, even if we assume that a machine makes an error while performing an entry, that error will only affect one copy, whereas we know that Blockchains keep several copies of the ledger across multiple locations and that each copy is consistently updated.

- **Decentralization** – By now, you must have known that Blockchains cannot be regulated by any single authority from a particular location.

In fact, the entire Blockchain is spread across several computers in a huge network in the form of multiple copies. Whenever any new data block is added or an existing block has to be deleted, all the nodes in the network modify their blockchains to reflect the change and keep the entire system up-to-date. Because of the absence of a single central database, you can't alter or damage any existing data easily. Tampering any existing data will occur only in one copy and not across the entire network, keeping the actual record intact and secure.

- **Efficient Transactions** – Whenever any central authority is involved in the transaction process, it will take a few days to complete. However, since Blockchains are running 24x7 the entire year through, you can perform any transaction in just a matter of a few minutes with complete security. This will help common people and businessmen who trade internationally and the existence of time zones, making the payment process extremely time-critical.

- **Security** – No wonder security is tight in a Blockchain. Any transaction, before getting listed needs to be verified by all the nodes in the network. After it is validated, it is added to the Blockchain as a new block. Every block has its unique hash value stored inside it, along with the hash value of the block immediately preceding it. It helps to maintain the sequence of the blocks correctly. Changes made to any existing block will also change its hash value but not the block's hash value next to it. Hence, any outsider cannot make a change without notifying the Blockchain network.

DRAWBACKS OF BLOCKCHAINS

- **Expensive** – Although Blockchains can remove the intermediate processing and transaction charges, the cost of setting up a Blockchain network is high. To constantly keep the system running and to facilitate 24x7 service, massive amounts of power are consumed. However, despite the huge costs involved in mining Bitcoin, more and more users prefer to validate transactions using mining computer rigs. Such users also receive an equivalent amount of Bitcoin as a reward to make their time and energy consumption worthwhile.

- **Illegal Activity** – Blockchain can prevent your data from hackers but can't stop illegal activity from taking place in the network. Because of its decentralized nature, users enjoy a massive amount of freedom to do whatever they like. The Blockchain has become a haven for dark web users and terrorists who trade in illegal goods using Bitcoin and other forms of crypto.

Therefore, Blockchains have both merits and demerits. However, many people argue that the pros of having a Blockchain network greatly outnumber its cons, given that most criminal activities occur under the nose of the government through untraceable cash.

WHAT IS CRYPTOGRAPHY?

Now, after studying Blockchains in detail, aren't you wondering how these individual blocks of information remain unique? The answer is simple. Blockchains involve a famous process known as cryptography to generate the unique hash values corresponding to each data block. Cryptography helps us secure information from outside view except for the involved parties. Any basic form of cryptography will involve an encrypting device, a key, and a decrypting device. Encryption algorithms take the original message and convert it into a ciphertext that is not in a human-readable form. The key allows the decrypting device to take the ciphertext as input and produce the original message as output in a human-readable format.

Most Blockchain applications are Public Blockchains and therefore don't involve sending secret, encrypted messages. However, Private and upcoming Blockchains utilize various cryptography algorithms to ensure security and maintain complete confidentiality of the information and the details. Some of the tools used in Blockchain cryptography that have several functionalities are hashing and digital signatures.

While hashing is used for creating a unique identification code for each data block, digital signatures help in verifying digital messages and documents. On the other hand, Hashing helps to maintain the immutability of the Blockchain. Cryptographic hashing doesn't involve the use of keys but rather a hash code generator that creates the required hash value for any given information of a specific length. SHA-256 cryptographic hash functions are blockchain technology's most commonly used hash functions.

The strength of an encoded message largely depends on the encryption algorithm used. Cryptography is what makes blockchains so secure and robust. Advanced and latest encryption algorithms make it harder for hackers to get inside the network and tamper with the data blocks. Only when all the nodes together call for a change, a data block is modified or created.

Therefore, it must be clear now how Blockchain and cryptography are related. You won't find isolated nodes in Blockchain networks because they operate on a peer-to-peer model. Therefore, blockchains have to maintain the correctness of the transactions along with ensuring their security on the unsecured channels. Consequently, cryptography is an integral part of every Blockchain in order to protect user information and privacy, as well as to maintain data consistency.

CHAPTER 3: WALLETS

Does your traditional wallet allow you to store Bitcoin? Or can you just fold it and put the Bitcoin in it? "The answer is No" since Bitcoins and other cryptocurrencies are not tangible, they don't have a physical form or shape. So they can't be stored physically in any traditional wallets. How about the crypto keys? Can we store them? How?

You can do this by using a digital crypto wallet. Let's take a look at what crypto wallets are, how to store your currency in one, and a lot more about them:

WHAT IS A DIGITAL WALLET?

A crypto wallet, which is often referred to as a digital wallet, is an application that allows any cryptocurrency user to store and retrieve their digital assets. It is used to store digital assets, just like we use conventional wallets to store our cash. You certainly do not need a wallet to spend your digital asset like in the case of fiat currency, but it nonetheless helps to store everything in one place. When you acquire any cryptocurrency, for instance, a Bitcoin, you can store it in your digital wallet, and from there, you can make the transactions.

The above was a brief overview of digital wallets, but to have a deeper understanding of them, consider them to be an application very similar to those which run on your computers or smartphones. If you prefer to experience the physicality of such a wallet, you can purchase a physical device that runs a wallet application similar to a USB device. So digital wallets can indeed be virtual or physical.

After the release of the Bitcoin protocol in 2009, Satoshi Nakamoto was the first to introduce the cryptocurrency wallet. Back then, Bitcoin was the most popular and frequently used cryptocurrency. But today, building upon blockchain technology, there are many other forms of cryptocurrencies, all of which can be stored together in a digital wallet. A digital wallet allows you to store multiple cryptocurrencies in one place.

There are two pairs of keys contained in a crypto wallet – public and private keys.

The first one is derived from the latter and functions as the address that is used to transfer cryptocurrencies to a wallet. The latter, or the private key, is quite similar to the key of a safe that you own. The private key is the most important part of the crypto wallet, and new users often find it difficult. You can only operate the wallet if you have access to your private key. Think of it as a bank account or a deposit box for cryptos, which requires a key to open.

As a result, access to the account is restricted and can only be accessed with an individual key that is distributed to you only.

So, in simple words, a public key acts as an address to your wallet, which others require to send the transaction to the wallet, whereas a private key acts as a password to open the wallet, so only you can access it.

Crypto wallets can be mainly classified into hardware and software wallets.

Software wallets are mainly browser extensions or computer programs. They facilitate traders by simplifying the process of storing and receiving crypto. They can even come in the form of mobile applications. A software wallet holds your private key online. In general, every type of cryptocurrency has its specific wallet. There are three types of software wallets –

- Desktop wallets that can be used on your laptop or computer, like the "Electrum wallet."
- Web-based wallets that work as browser extensions like "MetaMask."
- Mobile wallets like "blockchain.com wallets" where you can store currency and send or receive them. A user can sweep the private key

of any existing wallet into the application by using the QR code.

On the other hand, hardware wallets are small devices that can store your assets offline. Unlike software wallets, they keep your private keys off your phone or desktop. You will have to plug in the hardware wallet from the USB port to access the private key. Hardware wallets have a reputation for being more secure since you need to sign in from your hardware wallets by plugging them into your computer to access them.

There are three ways in which a hardware wallet can interact with your computer –

- An application created by a company
- A web-based interface
- A separate software wallet

People are still getting acquainted with cryptocurrency; however, crypto wallets are built in such a way that they can be easily operated by users. Wallets like Electrum and MetaMask are two of the most user-friendly wallets.

WHY IS WALLET IMPORTANT?

When you own an organization or company that holds a large amount of crypto, you need a third party to manage them, also known as a specialized custodian. If you are the single owner of the crypto, you need a non-custodial crypto wallet because, as mentioned earlier, your traditional wallet cannot store your crypto. Therefore, this is the main reason you need a digital wallet.

Your digital assets are stored on the Blockchain, but you need a private key to access them. The private key backs your asset on your non-custodial crypto wallet. A way of proving your ownership over your assets is your private key, and they are crucial in making transactions. It can also be considered as your wallet's password. Like the card security code to your credit cards, you need to keep this a secret and not tell anyone about it, as you may lose your money if you lose your key.

If you somehow forgot your private key, there is something called a seed phrase or a secret phrase. These phrases are twelve or twenty-four words that will function as your backup password. Remember to hide these phrases, and should anyone ever ask you to share these phrases with them, beware of the possibility of getting scammed.

Here's how to set up a crypto wallet. The task, however, is simpler than you may imagine. Setting up your crypto wallet will take you only a few minutes. If you want to have a software wallet, all you need to do is install the application that will support your assets. You can also install the browser extension on your smartphone. For instance, if you are using MetaMask, download the application, name your wallet, note down your seed phrase, and you are all done. Your wallet is now ready for transactions. You can send or receive funds. However, before choosing your wallet, a rule of thumb is to check that your crypto coin community supports it.

HOW TO SAFELY STORE YOUR COINS IN YOUR WALLET?

The cryptocurrency world may be new to you, so you need to be cautious, as one wrong step can result in losing your fortune. When you step into this space, you should know how to safely store your currency and operate it. You already know that digital crypto wallets are the way to store your currencies but do you know which wallet is the best? Let us look at the best option for you and how you can ensure the further safety of your cryptocurrency.

Hardware wallets, also commonly known as cold storage, are the safest method of storing your crypto coins. It is secure because it was designed by security experts and allows you to hold your private keys off the web. You can keep your private keys offline, nullifying the possibility of giving away access to anyone else. It will only be available to the holder of specific access codes. As mentioned above, you need to generate a set of private keys to use your hardware wallets, and you can store the keys offline. A four to eight-digit PIN will keep your wallet secure, and if there is an attempt of theft, the device will erase the PIN after several failed attempts.

However, remember that all hardware wallets are not the same. The level of security your hardware wallet will provide will solely depend on the features it provides you with. So, before you sign up with any provider, you should always dig into the features and see that the level of security it offers satisfies your needs.

These are a few criteria you must look for in any quality hardware wallet –

- **A PIN** – The PIN is the password with which you can access your wallet, and it should be known only by the owner.

- **A recovery phrase** – This is a code of up to twenty-four words. It stores every piece of information required to recover your wallet if it gets damaged, lost, or stolen. When anything unfortunate as this happens to your wallet, it does not mean you will no longer be able to access your coins. Hence, this is where the recovery phrase comes to use. It will help you access your crypto coins via a digital wallet or a new hardware wallet.

- **Security level** – By now, you have certainly understood the importance of having your wallet secured and protected, so when selecting a wallet, you would want to look out for one that has a high-quality security chip in it or is certified as one.

- **Ease of use** – The crypto ecosystem may be a complicated place for the newbies, so it is advisable to look for a wallet that is easy to use, enables you to directly control your assets, and gives you broad access to the crypto services that you are looking for.

HOW TO SECURE YOUR WALLET FROM HACKERS?

The threat to your crypto coins is mainly through your digital wallets. Any person who can enter your private key can perform fraudulent transactions on your currency. Following are some ways in which you can secure your cryptocurrency.

- **Use a non-custodial wallet** – In order to prevent your crypto holdings from being hacked, non-custodial wallets are the best, as they do not have the option of third-party access. At the same time, it puts the responsibility on you to safely store your keys. Make sure to have a good backup strategy. Most people will keep their keys on pen and paper and keep them safe. But, using a hardware wallet would give you an extra layer of protection due to its offline nature, which would give you even more protection. Due to this, it serves as a shield against malicious intent.

- **Avoid unregulated exchanges** – Not all exchanges are equally secure, and keeping your coins on unregulated ones is irresponsible. The reason is that the regulated ones have higher security standards than the unregulated ones, as the management behind most unregulated exchanges is faceless. In this case, if your fund gets lost, there are few repercussions.

- **Use a dependable internet connection** – Avoid Wi-Fi networks that are for public use while making crypto transactions. Use VPN while using your home network. The VPN will give you extra security. The VPN will change your IP address, location, and your browser activity will also be kept safe.

- **Secure your device** – Ensure that your device is updated and has anti-virus installed that can prevent vulnerabilities. Hackers then will not be able to take advantage of weak writing codes and attack your device.

- **Keep multiple wallets** – There is no limit to the number of wallets you can create, so consider diversifying your crypto assets in separate wallets. Maintain two wallets – one for regular transactions and another for storing the rest of your coins.

- **Change passwords regularly** – Nothing beats a strong password. Make sure to have complicated, strong passwords that cannot be guessed easily, and keep changing them regularly. Stop using the same password on multiple platforms. The password for all your wallets should be different.

- **Use MFA** – Multi-factor Authentication creates a layered defense of two or more independent credentials. It requires you to use multiple factors like passwords, security tokens, and biometrics that can provide stronger safeguards to your wallet. While setting up an MFA, you can select either Two-factor Authentication or push notifications. Sim swaps are common methods hackers use to attack wallets, so a 2FA is better since if hackers have access to your cloned sim card, they can easily steal your currency.

WHAT ARE THE BEST PLATFORMS TO BUY AND SELL CRYPTOCURRENCY?

If you already have crypto coins and are ready to invest or want to transfer money from your bank account and convert it to cryptocurrency, you will need a platform where you can perform these transactions. Below are some platforms that are the best for buying and selling cryptocurrency:

- **Coinbase** – This is the most popular and reliable cryptocurrency exchange, allowing users to invest directly in US dollars. On this platform, you can buy Bitcoins, Litecoins, Ethereum, and thirty other kinds of tokens. The platform is user-friendly and has a high level of security, which has earned its users' trust. The good selections of coins to invest in also make it popular among crypto users.

- **BlockFi** – This is an investment crypto platform where you can lend your holdings and earn interest. This platform enables you to borrow against your holdings instead of selling your coins. The platform is US-based and regulated. You can use it for free and earn a high-interest rate on your deposits.

- **Voyager** – The platform was one of the first to be publicly traded and is another popular crypto investment platform. The platform can be accessed through an application like BlockFi. You do not need to pay any commission. What makes the platform popular is that it supports major cryptocurrencies. It pays not only good rates on assets but also provides solid support and engagement.

- **Uphold** – Uphold is the go-to platform for trading multiple assets. Those who are regular crypto users will know that many coins can be traded only in pairs, so you would need to go back to ETH or BTC. But, with Uphold, you can open one account and trade multiple assets without switching between many exchanges. Uphold provides a transparent and simple pricing structure, which you can use from your smartphone and desktop.

- **Kraken** – This is one of the original platforms for crypto trading that supports a good number of crypto coins. This platform provides the facility of margin training. It is a complex exchange, which is why new users may not find it too easy, but it finds a place at the top list because it has high trust and security, supports a large variety of crypto, and allows for the trading of risky tokens like DOGE.

- **Crypto.com** – It is one of the fastest-growing crypto exchanges that is based in Hong Kong but is widely used by US-based customers. It enables its users to access more than ninety coins and tokens all over the world and around fifty tokens in the US.

Remember that a cryptocurrency wallet and a cryptocurrency platform or exchange are not the same. A digital wallet is a software that allows you to store your crypto coins, whereas an exchange is a website that facilitates trading cryptocurrency or converting fiat currency into cryptocurrency. Hence, crypto wallets were developed to keep your assets safe and secure since storing them on exchanges may expose them to theft.

CHAPTER 4: RISK MANAGEMENT

Cryptocurrency may be called the 'birth of a new era,' and the market has grown exponentially in the last few years. You have probably heard people say that investing in cryptocurrencies can make you filthy rich, which has encouraged more and more people to invest in them. Cryptocurrencies are indeed largely profitable, but this market comes with its own risks and challenges. The crypto market is volatile, and losses are also part of the package. Does that mean you should stop trading crypto assets altogether? Definitely not. Trading with caution can help you reap benefits without falling into the pit. This chapter will guide you to know the risks involved in crypto trading and safely investing in them.

WHAT ARE THE DIFFERENT KINDS OF RISK?

Cryptocurrencies are highly unpredictable as they, unlike fiat currencies, are not backed by the government or banks. All crypto transactions exist as digital entries on the Blockchain. The public ledger system is what makes it secure and trustworthy. Though the Blockchain may aid crypto security, there still remains risky, largely because of the decentralized nature of digital assets and the confidentiality it provides. The different kinds of risks that come with investing in cryptocurrency are as follows:

- **Volatility** – Volatility is the primary indicator of the financial health of any asset, and the most volatile assets in the markets are cryptocurrencies. The cryptocurrency market is fueled by speculators and investors like to trade assets just as they find a drop in the price. A single bad tweet about crypto can cause its price to plummet quickly. Recently, many investment firms have acquired noteworthy cryptocurrency stakes. The stabilizing influence of these companies could bring about healthy volatility in the crypto ecosystem.

- **Decentralization** – A feature that appeals greatly to the users is that no central authority is present, but it has its drawbacks too. For instance, most financial transactions are backed by a financial institution in the case of electronic money transfers. So, if any problem arises with the transaction, you can reach out to the institution and resolve it. But, with crypto transactions, it is not possible. Since there is no authority, there is no entity to resolve transaction disputes. This is why all crypto traders are advised to trade assets only through reputable exchanges. These exchanges provide great customer service, but the decentralized nature of crypto makes it difficult to resolve legal issues.

- **Peer-to-peer transactions and their risks** – A P2P (peer-to-peer) platform is a marketplace for cryptocurrency where crypto traders can connect personally with each other. All crypto transaction payments occur directly between the two parties on this platform. It is one of the best and easiest ways to convert cryptocurrency into fiat money. Here, you cannot rule out the possibility of negligence and mistakes causing you to lose your fortunes. The other risk that remains is that of scams where a buyer may not pay for crypto after it is transferred to them, or a seller may refuse to transfer the coins.

  Digital escrow service for P2P can be the only way of dodging fraudulent schemes. The platform, during the transaction holds the cryptocurrency, and the assets are released only after the buyer has completed the payment procedure and the seller confirms having received it. This way, both parties can prevent getting duped, and in case a problem arises, a representative of the platform will look into it.

- **Loss or destruction of private keys** – As you have already read in the previous chapter, crypto transactions use a system where a user needs a pair of keys to authenticate the transaction. There are two kinds of keys. The public key is available publicly, but only the user knows their private key, which they use as a password for authentication and identification. If you end up losing your private wallet key, it means that you lose access to your currency in the wallet.

About twenty percent of the time, Bitcoin losses occur when private keys are lost or get destroyed. It, therefore, becomes crucial to regularly backup your private keys and store them on an isolated device. Never store them online, especially if the format is not encrypted.

- **Unregulated trading platform exchanges** – It has become increasingly popular to trade cryptocurrency over the last few years, which has caused trading platforms and exchanges to grow in number. Because of this, it is now difficult for traders to choose a platform. In the crypto market, exchanges offer the same level of services as in the financial market, but an increase in fraudulent activities, scam exchanges, and market manipulation in crypto trading has been seen due to the lack of regulations. Predatory practices have increased in unregulated exchanges, and some trading exchanges charge hefty trading fees but do not have policies to prevent suspicious trading. Such weak security makes it easier for crooks to steal your assets.

Therefore, before signing up on any trading platform, always check their reviews and look into the security and guarantee they offer. Read the terms and conditions carefully to avoid getting caught in unrealistic claims.

- **Risks in currency conversion** – Cryptocurrencies are high-risk investments since their values fluctuate frequently. For instance, the price of Bitcoins climbed to its peak in December 2020 and fell by July next year. So, anyone who bought Bitcoins and traded them during that time would have made a good profit, whereas those who sold their coins after July would incur significant losses. The value of crypto fluctuates in relation to traditional currencies, and since they are speculative, crypto dealers have to depend on the value of the assets when they are trading them.

- **Regional regulations** –Regulations are a major menace to the growth of cryptocurrencies. The administrative authorities of different countries have imposed regulations to limit cryptocurrency usage in their respective nations. Crypto transactions are considered a way to circumvent several governments' financial transactions and money laundering.

Many countries at the moment are trying to figure out ways to integrate cryptocurrency with fiat currencies.

- **Taxation laws** – Since crypto-assets are considered capital assets, they are affected by the same laws applied to stocks. When one uses crypto to purchase and sell goods or barter them for services, they are affected by the capital gains tax as per the regulations of the IRS. Every cryptocurrency that we obtain through mining will also be subjected to taxes. Those who use cryptocurrencies need to submit their earning reports through crypto as income when filing their income tax as tax returns. However, the majority of crypto transactions are taxable, but not all of them are. Cryptos that are purchased, sold, stored, and exchanged through wallets are exempted from taxes. The laws of cryptocurrency can be confusing even for those who have gained some experience in this field.

- **Slowdown of network** - The process by which Bitcoins are generated, and transactions are verified is called mining. The computer of the user becomes a 'node' when they download specific software, and this node validates blocks where the details of some of the latest transactions can be found. Miners who can successfully add a block to the Blockchain get awarded Bitcoins automatically. However, the transaction fees or the reward that a user receives for solving blocks are low, and if a sufficient number of transactions occur simultaneously, the Blockchain slows down. If the number of transactions on the Blockchain is high, other cryptocurrencies may also experience this slowdown.

- **Loss of faith in digital currencies** – The digital asset industry is relatively new and is highly uncertain. Digital platforms used in the commercial and retail marketplace have made a gateway for trading activities by speculators who seek to make gains by holding cryptocurrencies for the long or short term. The majority of cryptocurrencies are neither backed by governments, central banks, or any other international organization. What determines the value of these currencies is the transactions that the participants of the market make. It implies that once there is a loss of confidence, the trading activities may crash, and there may be a significant drop in the value of the currencies.

- **'Fork' in the Blockchain** – Cryptocurrencies are based on protocols that govern the peer-to-peer interactions among several users. When users disagree about the protocols to be used, a 'fork' can result in opening two separate networks. For instance, in 2016, one such permanent fork on the Blockchain of Ethereum resulted in the creation of two separate versions of its digital currency, one being Ethereum classic or ETC and the other being Ethereum or ETH.

Not too long ago, Bitcoin two experienced a fork that resulted in the creation of a new cryptocurrency, Bitcoin Cash.

HOW CAN YOU MEASURE THESE RISKS?

The cryptocurrency mania has peaked worldwide due to its tremendous growth in the last few months. Experts say that the Blockchain will probably stay in the near future even if it does not entirely replace traditional currency anytime soon.

However, have you avoided it due to the risks?

Here is how you can measure or analyze the risks involved in crypto investments:

- **Sudden spurt in prices** – When a coin shows an increase in its price by a significant amount, you should take it as a warning signal. For instance, the Squid token was inspired after the famous series Squid Game was trading at around one percent, but the prices surged to two thousand dollars in less than seven days.

The best option is to invest in a stable version of a coin, as investing in these types will always involve risks.

- **Unrealistic promises** – Beware of such transactions when you find fancy promises of high investment returns that seem almost impossible. Remember that cryptocurrencies are volatile, and even those that have given good returns in the past cannot guarantee the same returns.

- **Dubious activity on social media handles** – Con artists sitting out there can hack the accounts of celebrities or famous personalities to attract investments. Watch out for such false testimonials and research the seller's background thoroughly before investing.

- **Validation requests through coins** – Cryptocurrency giveaways are good luring strategies for scammers. Even if you are asked to share only a small amount to avail of an offer or to validate an address, avoid falling for it.

- **Aggressive promotion** – If you find aggressive promotions on social platforms like YouTube or Telegram of a currency, beware. It could be a scam. Remember that if at any point you feel an offer is too good to be true, then it actually might not be true.

HOW TO MANAGE THE RISKS AND AVOID THEM?

Cryptocurrencies can be rewarding investments, but the risk factor involved can prompt many to back off. You can invest and trade crypto without losing your assets if you navigate your way safely.

Wondering how you can do that in what seems to be a maze laden with risks? Follow the tips below to manage and reduce the risks of investing in cryptocurrency:

- **Research** – Read, read and read. Nothing beats good research and knowledge. Just as you would read up and do your research before making any investment decision, do the same for cryptocurrencies. You may want to invest in crypto because some friend of yours has got good returns, or everyone around you is doing it, but it is always advisable to consult someone who has gained experience in this field before investing.

  Read the publication before making any cryptocurrency investment. That should give you a fair idea of the company's plans and an opportunity to judge if your plans align with them. Here, keep in mind that research done by someone else is not your research. You should do your own primary research. If you are a newbie, you might want to start off by reading up on digital assets before giving in to the temptation of investing in them. This is a crucial step, so do not be lazy as it may cost you your hard-earned fortune.

- **Gauge the reward/risk ratio** - The reward/risk ratio means how much profit you can make with every unit of currency you invest. Invest as per your capacity. Ideally, one should invest only what they can risk losing without having to end up in greater trouble because of it.

- **Diversify your portfolio** – The risk factor may be reduced if you invest in many crypto coins. The risk associated with the portfolio lessens as it diversifies. By investing across different coins, the impact of volatility can be minimized. Not all coins are equally volatile. Some are more fluctuating than others.

- **Define your strategy for entry and exit** – The essential part of your trade is your entry and exit. For a profitable trade, the icing on the cake would be a great entry, and at the exit, you will not only be looking at profits but also at losses. Planning when to exit is also an important part of a sound risk management strategy.

HOW TO WATCH OUT FOR THE IMPORTANT THINGS WHILE TRADING IN CRYPTO?

As an investor, you need to consider several factors before investing in cryptocurrencies and putting your money in them. Some of the things you should watch out for or consider before trading in crypto are –

- **Identify the right investment** – Not all investments in crypto will be profitable. An investor needs to first understand the market evaluation. Make an informed decision after considering the market capitalization and estimating the value of crypto. Identify the coins that have potential and can skyrocket anytime.

- **Check legitimacy** – Make sure to look up the seller's background, which may tell you whether the asset is genuine or not. Experts say that instead of investing in crypto that got launched recently and whose owners aren't well-known, it is better to invest in one that has been around for a year or two in the market.

- **Understand the value proposition** – When considering what project to invest in, investors should consider the project's history and purpose. Understanding the project value proportion is essential. Also, try to find out the gap that the project is trying to fill.

- **Compare the price trend in relation to the market trend** – When looking at a particular cryptocurrency, analyzing the price trend in relation to the market gives one clarity over investments and the potential they may have in the future.

Investing in cryptocurrency involves great risks, and all traders in this ecosystem should prepare themselves for it eventually. The lack of authority and decentralized nature makes it all the more vulnerable, giving an opportunity to con artists. As a beginner in crypto investing, I recommend investing only what you are prepared to lose without suffering significant repercussions if you fail.

CHAPTER 5: PORTFOLIO ANALYSIS

Crypto, a new rage, is taking over the world, and now is the perfect time to get involved. But you do not know where to start, do you?

To start your crypto journey, you would need to build a crypto portfolio. Before we learn how to build one, let us first understand what a crypto portfolio is and its purpose.

The term crypto portfolio refers to a collection of cryptocurrencies that belongs to a crypto trader or an investor who owns them. Typically, there are a variety of assets contained in a portfolio, including not only crypto financial products but also altcoins. A crypto portfolio is very much like a traditional investment portfolio that you may be familiar with. The only difference is that you stick to one asset in crypto portfolios. A crypto portfolio serves as the means to your inventory of online currency investments. This can be considered as a profit and loss statement, which helps traders keep a stock of their assets.

HOW CAN YOU BUILD A CRYPTO PORTFOLIO?

Wondering how you can build a solid portfolio for your crypto assets? Here are four easy steps to guide you in building your crypto portfolio.

- **Learn the basis of crypto investing** – The world of crypto is relatively new, and jumping into this vast sea without the basic knowledge of crypto and how it works can land you in the deep end. Cryptocurrencies are decentralized digital currencies, and they operate on Blockchains. It was the introduction of Bitcoin in January 2009 that started the crypto movement. In the past decade, the crypto ecosystem has flourished to become a thriving asset market where even investors have equal opportunities.

    Are you wondering if you should then change your current fiat investment strategy? Well, not really. Nevertheless, it is always a good idea to do your own research and determine which currency will be the best fit for you. You can use applications like Voyager that act as a broker and continue to invest through them. Even while using such applications, you can use the dollar-cost averaging strategy whereby you can limit orders as well as limit recurring buys to invest steadily and make the most of your investment.

The basics of investing are very much alike, but the difference in growth becomes apparent when you discover how easier and simpler crypto makes it to diversify, build, and maintain a thriving portfolio.

- **Explore the various types of cryptocurrencies** – Cryptocurrencies and Bitcoins are almost synonymous terms in the mainstream crypto world today since Bitcoins are one of the most widely known type of cryptocurrency. Today, there are more than nine thousand altcoins available on the crypto market. All other types of cryptocurrencies barring Bitcoins, are known as altcoins.

    Altcoins have added diversity to crypto offerings and, as a result, have created different crypto sectors. USD coin, for instance, is a stable coin that is matched with the US dollar and allows you to earn around nine percent of rewards annually if you hold a USD coin on Voyager. DeFi, or decentralized finance, is another popular sector of crypto that will allow you to lend, borrow, and exchange through decentralized platforms. Altcoins also range across a vast number of interests from sports, entertainment, and gaming as well.

- **Choose crypto assets based on performance and investment horizon** – The crypto market is abundant with assets making it difficult for newbies to decide which they should include in their portfolio. With so many options at hand, you may easily get confused not knowing where you should begin. Safe players like to begin their crypto journey with well-known picks like Ethereum and Bitcoin. You, too, could choose that path. Both these assets have been around for more than a year and have built a steady reputation in the market. Since altcoins are newer and are yet to gain prominence in the market, you will have to keep an eye on their performance if you want to invest in them. Study their trade volume, market caps, and planned network upgrades. These statistics will come in handy to determine how many coins are available for a specific asset and how they are being traded, giving you a fair idea of how they would yield in the future.

  Some investors like to invest and hold on to their assets without selling them because the crypto market is volatile. This can prove beneficial on several platforms as they help you earn rewards on your investment. For instance, it is possible to earn annual rewards on Voyager if you hold assets like Polkadot in the application.

The nature of crypto makes it possible for investors to buy assets in fractions. This basically means that if you are not ready to buy one whole Bitcoin, you can buy some of it; this offers you a scope to experiment with buying assets. Since the very beginning, the crypto market has been volatile, and due to this nature of the market, there is every chance for one to buy an asset when they are at a lower value. The decentralized aspect of the crypto market in this manner provides an opportunity for all.

- **Use apps to store and track your crypto portfolio** – There are a few applications that are creating an alternative to monitoring and tracking crypto wallets and crypto platforms. One such application is Voyager. On Voyager, you can store your crypto portfolio as well as monitor all your assets in real-time, and all of this can be done only with a few swipes. There are presently more than six hundred assets you can choose from, and more are being added often. There are over thirty assets that offer annual rewards of up to twelve percent if you hold a monthly minimum balance in the app.

WHAT DO YOU MEAN BY ASSET ALLOCATION?

The meaning of asset allocation is splitting up an investment portfolio into different categories of assets. It depends on the personal choice of the trader as to what mix of assets they want to hold in their portfolios. The two factors which will determine the asset allocation that will be best suited for you are – the time horizon and how much risk you are willing to take.

But why is it so important? It is because when a single portfolio comprises crypto categories along with investment returns and the value of which keeps increasing or decreasing under different conditions, the trader can be protected from incurring huge losses. It is the market conditions that regulate the performance of an asset. When you invest in several asset categories, the risk of losing money gets reduced automatically. The overall investment returns of your portfolio, too, are bound to be in better shape. Even if the investment of one category of asset sinks, you will be in a good position to prevent your losses in another asset category with better returns.

WHAT IS PORTFOLIO REBALANCING?

Investors for decades have been using the strategy of portfolio rebalancing. When you implement rebalancing as a strategy for your portfolio, it implies that you will have to determine how much of your portfolio you want to dedicate to each of your assets. The same goes for your crypto portfolio, where each asset would mean a token. They show the percentage of each asset that must find representation in the total value of the portfolio when combined. In order to rebalance the portfolio, these assets are traded so that their value reaches the initial specified percentage.

Let us try to understand with the help of an instance. Let us say that your portfolio contains four crypto assets – ETH, XMR, BTC, and LTC. Your wish is that these coins take up identical stakes in your portfolio. It means that each crypto gets a twenty-five percent stake, and your portfolio at the end of rebalancing would contain twenty-five percent of these assets. Coins generally do not have the same value, which is why the calculation of the value should be made either in base or in fiat currency. Therefore, the coins will be different in quantity. This means that if you have a total of a hundred dollars between the four assets in your portfolio, you would have twenty-five dollars in each at the end of the rebalancing.

But why do you need to rebalance your portfolio? With the trend of crypto investors holding investments, which means not selling or trading crypto with the intention of making future profits, rebalancing creates a scope to increase the earnings that are on hold by using the rapid fluctuations in market price to advantage. When a coin generates good returns, the gains from it will be distributed among the other crypto assets when rebalanced. This means that rebalancing will allow the portfolio to maintain a positive gain over the period even if the returns come back to the price, it was before the increase.

There are mainly three common crypto portfolio rebalancing strategies –

- **Periodic rebalancing** – This is a very straightforward and time-based approach to resizing your investments. You will have to decide on an initial investment allocation between various crypto coins and tokens. After a fixed period of hours, days, or weeks, your portfolio assets will be sold or bought in the necessary proportions to return to the desired asset allocation. Even if your portfolio is out of balance on the basis of percentage, rebalancing will occur only once the time period is reached.

- **Percentage portfolio rebalancing** – This balancing strategy defines absolute percentage-based allocations to investment based on a range of acceptable deviations. If the crypto you own falls or rises past the target amount and the tolerated range, the trade rebalances the entire portfolio back to your desired allocation.

- **Threshold rebalancing** – You will have to set an initial target allocation and a percentage of deviation from those target levels that serve as the 'threshold.'

HOW TO REBALANCE YOUR PORTFOLIO?

Portfolio rebalancing is a strategic tool that helps crypto traders safeguard against overexposure to unplanned risk. Here is a step-by-step guide that will help you to rebalance your crypto portfolio.

Step 1 – Decide which type of rebalancing strategy will suit your investment style

Your investment strategy and style will play a big role in determining the type and duration of necessary portfolio rebalancing. Investments that are of higher risk like coins that have been newly launched, volatile coins, or those with limited market capitalization. Such assets generally require more balancing than a portfolio that contains one or two stable currencies and a single high-risk token or at the most two. Figure out which balancing strategy will fit well with your unique investment plan as well as your risk tolerance before moving on to the starting allocation of your investment.

Step 2 – Assign your starting crypto-asset allocation

Determine the initial investment mix and balance. If you have already begun trading, you will have to divide up your existing portfolio into the crypto asset allocation based on your risk management strategy and the assets you own. For instance, an investor may hold up to forty percent of their portfolio value in a large market capitalization cryptocurrency like BTC, twenty percent in ETH, and the rest forty percent invested in two ICOs and two altcoins evenly.

Step 3 – Rebalance your cryptocurrency portfolio

Suppose you are rebalancing your portfolio based on a periodic strategy schedule. In that case, buying and selling the crypto assets needed to reach your predetermined investment allocation. you can alternatively use portfolio or threshold rebalancing. Threshold rebalancing would involve setting a percentage deviation from your allocation that you do not want to be breached. Percentage rebalancing adjusts allocations based on absolute changes in your percentage.

Step 4 – Make the trades

It is suggested that you purchase and sell the crypto assets that would allow you to get back to your original cryptocurrency asset allocation goal. If you are not using any crypto portfolio balancing tool and rebalancing it manually, you will need to try to ensure that transactions are executed in a timely manner. You will also be required to log each transaction to compare investment performance at a later stage accurately and to track capital gains for tax purposes if you are in the US. All rebalancing transactions must be recorded in accordance with your local tax laws.

WHAT IS FUNDAMENTAL ANALYSIS OF CRYPTOCURRENCY MARKETS?

In order to determine the variables that can play a role in affecting a value, traders can use this tool to assess and evaluate the factors. The device mainly studies facts and factors that can have an impact on the value of the asset. Fundamental analysis has proved to be extremely useful in analyzing the market along with technical analysis, as its focal point is to figure out how the value of the security may be affected by external factors. In analysis, technically, the focus is mainly on standing market charts to anticipate values.

Mainly there are two types of approaches that strive to offer the best response to the trader. The approaches are thought of as analyzing macro and microeconomic variables in one way or another. The two types of approaches are –

1. **Top-down approach** – In this approach, first the macroeconomic variables are looked into, and then the microeconomic variables. It means that global information is taken into account, addressing the detailed and specific values, and only then are decisions made.

2. **Bottom-up approach** – In this approach, the microeconomic variables are first focused on and then macroeconomic variables are

considered. Unlike the top-down approach, this offers a more specific vision.

In the context of the crypto market, the fundamental analysis allows for analyzing the extrinsic factors. Due to the ever-fluctuating nature of the market, which reacts instantly to these factors. For instance, the administrative pressures from countries like China, USA, and other European nations significantly impact the price of cryptocurrencies. Such events make fundamental analysis important as it helps to realize the real value of a crypto asset.

Some of the factors observed by the fundamental analysis of cryptocurrencies are –

- **Usability and adoption** - A cryptocurrency's real value will increase as it becomes more widely adopted.

- **Position of government and regulations** – The aim of studying this point is to check the reaction of the government to a certain cryptocurrency and if the asset is in compliance with governmental regulations or not.

- **Project development and its media coverage** – The development activity of cryptocurrency, the exchange platform it uses, and an increase in the media coverage it gets will show the true potential of a cryptocurrency and that it has the ability to generate a greater amount of value in the future.

Crypto is still an emerging asset class that is rapidly expanding. If you want to be an investor, you will need to possess knowledge about the digital asset ecosystem. Hopefully, this chapter has helped you to learn more about crypto portfolios. Balancing your portfolio does not only mean possessing a multitude of coins. Strategizing a bit will take you a long way in structuring a portfolio that will be suitable to your risk appetite.

CHAPTER 6: HOW TO INVEST IN CRYPTOCURRENCIES?

The cryptocurrency market currently has over six thousand cryptocurrencies, but does that mean that every single one of them is worth buying? No, just as not all fiat currencies are on the same level, cryptocurrencies, too, in the same way, are not equally valuable. Suppose you are an investor looking to enter the crypto world. In that case, you may have many questions, and the first few of them surely are – if you should buy large amounts of the same currency, divide your money between two currencies, or invest in multiple currencies.

As a matter of fact, no one formula fits everybody's requirements, and your decision to invest in the type and amount of cryptocurrencies will majorly depend on your risk appetite. Specific cryptocurrencies serve specific needs, such as app developers, investors, day traders, etc. In order to make informed investment decisions, it is always advised to have a deeper understanding and knowledge of digital currencies.

HOW TO FIND AND CHOOSE BETWEEN TOP CRYPTOCURRENCIES IN THE MARKET?

When you enter the crypto market as an investor, you will be overwhelmed with choices to invest in. But, the first question that will come to your mind before making a crypto investment is which currency you should invest in among the many at hand since the majority of them look enticing. The answer to your question would be "Research." To find out the best investment options for your needs, you will need to look up the following things:

- **Age and enthusiast trust** – In the end, what makes the difference between a cryptocurrency that becomes popular and one that sinks without a trace is the community that grows around the cryptocurrency and the trust that the community builds in it.

- **Blockchain generation** – As cryptocurrencies are divided into two categories - coins and tokens - the newer generation of cryptocurrencies allows users to unlock more possibilities in the future thanks to the underlying blockchain technology.

- **Supply conditions** – It's really important to consider how the limited or unlimited supply of a currency can have a substantial impact on how a currency can be used and what impact it can have on the wider economic ecosystem in the long run.

- **Specialty** – Each currency, over a time period, settles into a different niche.

- **Value and visibility** – To put it simply, transaction pricing provides advantages such as the ability to divide a hundred-dollar piece of currency into hundred notes of a dollar each and to further subdivide it into a hundred coins of one penny each. Cryptocurrencies, in the same way, can be divided into hundreds of sub-units allowing for flexibility in transactions.

- **Transaction costs** – Whenever you are involved in a transaction, there will always be an element of expense involved, but the only real question is whether you will lose three percent or one percent in the transaction.

- **Transaction speed** – Essentially, this would be the same as waiting in line at the check-out counter. As soon as a sale or purchase is made, you will want the cashier to confirm your sale or purchase as soon as possible.

- **Perceived transaction privacy** – In the crypto ecosystem, currencies can be perceived to allow for different levels of privacy, yet it is still possible for law enforcement authorities to investigate most of the transactions that take place using the cryptocurrency.

Remember that external and intangible factors are greatly responsible for how a currency performs in the long run and its performance compared to other currencies.

Currently, the most profitable cryptocurrencies and the ones that are currently ruling the market are the following:

- **Bitcoin** – The value of Bitcoin has skyrocketed in the last few years and has become a household name. Due to its popularity, it has become synonymous with the term cryptocurrency. It has survived for over a decade and continues to dominate the market with a capitalization of around nine hundred billion dollars.

- **Ethereum** – In addition to being a cryptocurrency, it is also a blockchain platform and can be called the golden counterpart to Bitcoin. Its potential applications make it a favorite among program developers and a popular spot for high-value trades such as Nfts.

- **Tether** – The great thing about Tether is that it is a stablecoin, which means that it is backed by fiat currencies like the Euro or U.S. dollar, as opposed to many other cryptocurrencies. Therefore, Tether is supposed to be more consistent when compared to other cryptocurrencies and this is a reason why many investors prefer it.

- **U.S. Dollar Coin or USDC** – Just like Tether, this is also a stablecoin, and the price is set at 1 USDC for 1 USD.

WHAT STRATEGIES CAN YOU FOLLOW FOR CRYPTO TRADING?

The crypto market is laid with fraud mines, and as a trader, you may have to face several stumbling blocks. To enjoy benefits that will last longer and ensure you have a fun and secure ride in this ever-evolving market, you need to have an effective strategy.

- **Day trading** – For this strategy, an investor is required to take a position and exit the position on that very day. When booking a trade like this, the trader must book with the aim of booking profits and price movements for the selected cryptocurrency over the course of the day. Technical indicators can be relied on in this case to find out the entry and exit points of a particular crypto coin.
- **Range trading** – Not just newbies but also traders with experience depend on analysts who can provide them with resistance and support levels on a daily basis. The maximum point to which the price of crypto may rise is termed the resistance level, which means that it is a price

above the current price. The level below which the price of crypto is not supposed to fall is termed the support level. It means that the support level is almost never above the current price. An investor should find out both ranges of cryptocurrency before making a purchase.

- **Scalping** – This is a strategy of trading where the volumes of trades are increased in order to reserve a profit. Even though this is a little risky, it is possible for a market player to tackle the margin requirement and other regulations so that they do not have to face an unpleasant experience when trading. Scalpers, within a day, make an analysis of the cryptocurrencies, the trends of the past, and volumes, and make a choice about the entry and the exit point.

- **HFT** – It stands for High-Frequency Trading, which is a strategy that is algorithmic and primarily used by quantitative traders. This process entails the development of algorithms and exchanging bots. The main function of these bots is to help one to enter and exit any cryptocurrency. One needs to understand the complicated concepts of the market as well as be knowledgeable about both computer science and mathematics to be able to develop such bots.

- **Dollar-cost averaging** – Timing the market is a difficult task and almost impossible, so investing in cryptos in Dollar-Cost Averaging is a sound way. It includes investing fixed amounts at regular intervals. This strategy helps to mitigate the unmanageable task of timing the market.

- **Build a balanced portfolio** – The crypto market is volatile, you already know that by now, but by building a strong portfolio containing a variety of cryptocurrencies, you may be able to beat the volatility factor. Having a balanced portfolio will also ensure that you can invest a fixed amount regularly in crypto assets of your choice. This will also gradually increase your appetite for risk creating scope for gaining returns that would be favorable in the long run.

- **Primary research** – Of all strategies, the most important one is to research. Researching an asset you want to trade doesn't require you to be an expert in the field. It is important to stay up-to-date on all the crypto industry news as part of primary research. Two things you must do before putting your money on crypto are to judge and evaluate your finances and have a fixed target for investment in your mind.

- **Arbitrage** – The term arbitrage is used to refer to the strategy whereby a crypto trader sells their asset in another market and not in the same one they had bought it from. The balance that remains between the buying and selling price of the crypto is termed 'spread.' Traders can find an opportunity to book a profit owing to the difference in liquidity and trading volume.

HOW TO DETERMINE THE VALUE OF CRYPTOCURRENCY?

The factors that are instrumental in determining the value of digital currencies are –

- **Cryptocurrency public ledger** - The technology that works behind cryptocurrencies plays a very important role in determining their price. Since these assets are digital, it is possible for coding bugs to be present. Dao, a smart contract that is Ethereum based, once had a bug that a hacker exploited and made more than thirty million dollars from it. To fix this problem, some wanted a change in the blockchain while others did not, and as a result, Ethereum was split into two sections – Ethereum and Ethereum Classic. An event of this kind is termed a 'fork,' and it can cause an impact on the value of cryptocurrencies.

- **Node count** - It is one more element that enhances the value of the digital currency. It is also an indicator that shows how many wallets are active on the network. This can be found by searching on the homepage of crypto. It helps to show if a coin is overbought.

- **Rising demand** - Supply and demand are important factors determining the value of anything that can be traded, and crypto-assets are no exception. The rising demand for cryptocurrencies can cause their prices to spike. For instance, if more people try to buy Bitcoins, automatically, their prices will increase, while if their demand decreases, their prices will fall.

- **Mass adoption** – It is possible for the value of a currency to shoot through the roof if it gains mass adoption. A reason for this is that the summation of most cryptocurrencies has a short supply. Their price naturally increases when their demand is higher. As far as acceptance and adoption of cryptocurrency are concerned, it depends on how many places will actually accept cryptocurrencies as digital payments, or how applicable they are in real-life scenarios. If a crypto asset finds use as fiat assets do in our everyday lives, it can acquire a significant position in the upcoming days.

- **Expansion of fiat currencies** – In the event that the price of fiat currency crashes, there is no doubt that Bitcoin's price will increase with regard to fiat currency. The reason for this is that by using your Bitcoins, you will be able to access more of the fiat currency.

- **Production cost** – The direct and opportunity costs are also factors that play a role in determining the value of a crypto coin. For instance, the cost of production of Bitcoins is high. It can be said that Bitcoin's high value is the result of the power and resources that go into mining it.

- **Regulation** – Once crypto assets go mainstream, the chance for regulation by the governments is high. Digital money could become centralized with these regulations, and that may impact the price of the cryptocurrency.

WHICH ARE THE BEST PLATFORMS FOR TRADING CRYPTOCURRENCY?

Now that you have gained some decent knowledge about digital assets and are familiar with trading strategies, you may be wondering where you can start trading. Some of the best platforms for trading cryptocurrencies are –

- **Coinbase** – It is by far the most popular platform. One of the best features of this exchange platform is the possibility of investing directly with U.S. dollars. This platform currently allows the trade of Ethereum, Bitcoins, Litecoins, and thirty more varieties of digital coins. The platform owes its popularity for its easy interface, high level of security, good selection of tokens, and trustworthiness.

- **Voyager** – This is another popular crypto exchange platform that is driven by an app, offering a commission-free trading structure. Voyager supports most major cryptocurrencies and provides solid interest rates. Again, this too has a very easy-to-use interface making it popular among new investors.

- **Binance** – Launched in 2017, this Malta-based exchange is popular among digital investors globally. This exchange charges less than one percent on trades and offers its users the option to earn interest on their coins by stacking them for a while. This exchange offers good security and has an asset fund as assurance in case a user's funds are stolen. There are more than fifty varieties of coins available on this platform.

- **Kraken** – It is one of the oldest and original crypto platforms, which is why you will find a good selection of coins to trade or invest in. They are among those few platforms that grant the facility to trade risky crypto tokens such as DOGE and a few others.

- **Crypto.com** – Based in Hong Kong, it gives a lot of support to U.S based customers and is among the most popular crypto exchanges. Currently, it offers access to more than ninety coins and tokens worldwide and around fifty tokens for U.S. customers. They also are known for offering solid rates on their crypto savings account.

- **eToro** – Previously available only in the UK and Europe, this platform is now allowing traders in the US to trade. The exchange also offers a wide selection of coins.

WHAT DO YOU UNDERSTAND BY VALUE INVESTING?

It is a strategy of investment that entails using fundamental analysis to find stocks that seem to be selling at a lower price than their book value. Investors actively find stocks they think are being underestimated by the market. It is believed that the market overreacts to both good and bad news. This causes the stock price to fluctuate, which is not in line with the company's long-term fundamentals. One can take advantage of this situation and make a profit by buying stocks either on sale or at a discounted price. The concept that goes on behind value investing is quite simple. One can save quite a bit of their money if they know the real price of something and then purchase it on sale. I believe a majority of people do not care whether you buy an appliance for the full price or on sale as long as you do not sacrifice the quality of the product. Stocks work in a similar pattern and the same goes with crypto. It implies that the price of a coin can change even though its valuation of it might not have changed. To put it simply, value investing is the process of looking out for coins that are undervalued so that you can buy them at a price lower than what the market values them.

Given the instability of the market, investing in cryptocurrency is considered risky. They are considered more volatile than stocks. The high returns that you hear can lure you into joining the bandwagon of crypto trading, but you should never do it because others are doing it. Before you start investing, it is advised that you research the basics of this ecosystem and the digital coin you want to invest in. Carefully note the fee for a transaction when purchasing crypto, as the difference between these fees is quite vast between the different currencies.

CHAPTER 7: HOW TO TRADE CRYPTOCURRENCY?

A Contract for Difference (CFD) is a method of computing currency price changes in trading accounts. During CFD settlements, opening and closing trades are compared, and Digital coins are traded as commodities. These include Bitcoin, Ethereum, Dogecoin, and many others. This involves profit from short, medium, or long-term rise and fall prices.

HOW IS BLOCKCHAIN USED?

Cryptocurrency trading involves blockchain technology specializing in trading strategies and the digital marketplace. A blockchain keeps track of all kinds of transactions, not just financial transactions, and the information contained in the blockchain adds to the ability to keep track of anything with intrinsic value. The records stored are permanent and contain timestamps. These timestamps are controlled by a group of hardware systems. The blockchain also contains information or blocks which are cryptographically encrypted.

In cryptocurrencies, verifying transactions is essential; There is a process in blockchain technology called mining. Through this process, people can generate more cryptocurrency coins in the blockchain network. The people who perform mining are called miners, and along with the generation of new coins, mining also serves another purpose. Miners, during mining, are required to compete with one another to decode a hash, which is a mathematical equation, and the first miner to do so gets to add blocks on the blockchain, along with the reward of receiving coins.

TRADING CRYPTOCURRENCY

Cryptocurrency trading is the process by which individuals can buy, sell or trade cryptocurrencies in the blockchain network. There are three main aspects of cryptocurrency trading. These include the items to be sold, which can include any cryptocurrency assets like coins or tokens, and buying and selling strategy. A buying and selling strategy could be any method that traders use to ensure that they sell as many cryptocurrency assets as possible, making the highest amounts of profit. Some may use the help of an investor to achieve their goal of maximizing their profit.

There are over thousands of cryptocurrencies that are being used in the blockchain network, but the most famous of them all is called Bitcoin. It first came into being in 2019. Since then, it has taken the digital world by storm and today is ranked as one of the highest-selling cryptocurrencies in the world.

Another popular cryptocurrency is Litecoin. It was developed in 2011 by Charlie Lee, and its aim was to provide a platform for cheaper transactions and more suitable for regular use.

HOW TO DO A TECHNICAL ANALYSIS TO FIND OUT WHAT ARE THE BEST MARGINS, OPTIONS, AND FUTURE?

Just like before starting any business, the most important thing is to do market research and lay down all the facts; similarly, before you start trading cryptocurrencies, it is extremely important to do technical analysis. This will help you in predicting the highs and lows of the crypto market. This is going to make all your decisions based on hard facts which are supported by data.

CRYPTOCURRENCY TRADING STRATEGY

There are two main trading tactics used for cryptocurrency trading. These are termed technical and fundamental. The similarity between the two is that they both depend on qualitative data to validate their effectiveness.

Recently, a new type of trading approach, known as quantitative trading, has gotten a lot of attention. This type of approach depends upon the information received through transactions from the cryptocurrency platforms to create trading choices. Quantitative traders use quantitative data, which is usually acquired from the price, volume, technical indicators, ratios, and form. Since most of the trading strategies are automated, the user does not have to perform them manually.

The difference between cryptocurrency marketplaces and traditional ones is that the former offers more profit-making opportunities, has higher volatility, and is more transparent. Because of these qualities, most traders and analysts in cryptocurrency markets prefer to use quantitative trading tactics.

An encompassing term called systematic trading is used to define a large number of activities related to cryptocurrency trading, such as controlling risks, following rules, and having a clear idea of trading goals. Systemic trading is not a fast type of investment.

Cryptocurrencies are developed using many different tools, including Machine Learning. This type of tool emphasizes two features. One is the input features, and the other is the objective function. When we say input features, we talk about the sources of data. The effect of both fundamental and technical knowledge impacts the input features. It can be classified into more than one type, such as economic indicators, social indicators, technical indicators, and seasonal indicators, all of which include different types of information and data.

In machine learning, there are three types: Supervised, Unsupervised, and Reinforcement Learning.

Labeled data is used in supervised learning. On the other hand, unsupervised learning uses unlabeled training data. As the name suggests, unlabeled data is a data set that has not been tagged with labels, properties, characteristics, or classifications that would help differentiate it from the rest. On the other hand, labeled data has to identify characteristics or tags that help to identify it from others. Reinforcement learning uses software to carry out the learning process. These software agents serve utility functions, which help to define their objectives.

HOW TO AVOID COMMON MISTAKES THAT MOST TRADERS MAKE

When it comes to trading in cryptocurrency, nobody is certain about anything. People make mistakes and learn from them. Let's examine a few ways to avoid making some common mistakes; avoiding these will give you a distinct advantage over your competitors.

- ***Portfolio Theory***

    By carefully distributing assets, portfolio theory encourages users to make different types of investments to get the maximum percentage of returns. There are a few typical methods for constructing a diversified crypto-asset portfolio. One of the techniques is to expand across markets. Another way is to research the relevant industries and know more about the different areas in which you can invest to avoid putting too much money into one area.

- ***Market Condition Research***

    For cryptocurrencies, market research is extremely critical. A financial bubble occurs when the cost of equity rises dramatically without changing its intrinsic value. Several experts believe there was a bitcoin bubble in 2017 when cryptocurrency values increased by 900 percent. In 2018, the value of Bitcoin plummeted. Researchers have been studying bitcoin trading bubbles and difficult situations as a result of this huge fluctuation.

- ***Short-Term Investment***

Given the unstable nature of the market, investors should consider crypto as a long-term investment. The crypto industry is still developing and uncertain because new builds are continuously being tested. The market might be flourishing one minute and then failing the next. One can get better results if one avoids short-term rewards and goes with a long-term approach.

- **Secure Trading Platform**

    The first and most obvious rule is to use cryptocurrency exchanges that are reliable, safe, and stable. Many illegalities and frauds are being performed through bogus crypto exchanges due to the increased popularity and development of the cryptocurrency platforms and the high number of users who are ready to invest in them. So you should care enough not to invest in a fraud cryptocurrency platform whose sole intention is to rob you of your money.

- **Fat-Finger Error**

    When an investor makes a fat-finger error, meaning that they accidentally enter a trading order that isn't what they intended. A single missing zero can result in enormous losses, and even a single decimal place can have severe consequences. It is always a good idea to double check the values.

- **Over Diversification**

    Diversification is essential for developing a stable cryptocurrency portfolio, especially given the market's extreme volatility. However, due to the wide variety of options available and the widespread desire for large returns. *Comma?* Cryptocurrency investors frequently over-diversify their investments, which can have disastrous repercussions. Over-diversification can result in a large number of underperforming assets being held by one investor, resulting in considerable losses. It's critical to diversify into cryptocurrencies only when the underlying value is evident and to have a thorough understanding of the many sorts of assets and how they'll likely perform in different market conditions.

- **Setting up a Stop-Loss**

    A stop-loss order allows investors to sell an investment only if the market hits a predetermined price. Investors use this to ensure that they do not lose more money than they are prepared to lose and that they at least recoup their initial investment. Investors had lost a lot of money in the past because they set their stop losses erroneously before asset prices collapsed. It's also crucial to realize that stop-loss orders aren't flawless, and in the event of a massive, rapid drop, they may fail to trigger a sale.

SUPPLY AND DEMAND

It is a well-known fact that supply and demand always go hand in hand when it comes to the fundamentals of trading. Even in our day-to-day lives, we often find ourselves looking for the best deal when we set out to make a purchase, and similarly, when we try to sell something to someone, we often find ourselves trying to maximize the profits. This same theory runs in almost every possible trading venture, even in cryptocurrency trading. It is often seen that early traders, who lack expertise and experience, are comfortable with selling their shares or cryptocurrencies at a discounted price if they have been holding on to them for too long and want to get rid of them. At the same time, professional traders are constantly looking to acquire them wholesale and resell them at retail, making profits. A transfer of funds from inexperienced accounts to professional accounts usually occurs from time to time. And the term used to describe the location where this occurs is called a supply or demand zone.

In order to identify a supply or demand zone, the price of a cryptocurrency must move from one specific location to another on the chart. This price variation associated with the movement can be properly analyzed using comprehensive charts and monitoring tools used for the purpose. When this movement occurs, it implies that there was a purchasing or selling interest at the time of its occurrence. Once this occurs, one must wait for the price to revert so that we can potentially purchase or sell at a discounted rate.

Supply zones, on the other hand, are comparable to resistance levels in their behavior. They are, once again, wider, but the price tends to fall after they are reached. Several factors need to be considered when it comes to supply and demand to trade.

There is a theory called Wyckoff's "accumulation and distribution" theory. This theory takes us through the creation of trends. According to the theories, prior to the beginning of a trend, the price remains in an "accumulation" zone as long as the "big players" have taken up their locations and then make the price go high.

To have a good supply zone, there are certain factors that need to be present, such as:

Moderate Volatility: In order to have a good zone of supply, it is necessary for it to have a narrow price behavior. If a supply zone on a graph has too many back-and-forth motions, it is canceled and considered to be not a good one. If the supply zone is narrower, just prior to a strong breakout, the chances of a positive reaction are more for the next time.

Exits: Having the price for too long in a supply zone is not what you would want, as a general rule. As previously said, good supply zones are narrower and don't last very long.

HOW TO EVALUATE CRYPTO TECHNOLOGIES?

The following systems will assist you in evaluating technologies:

Trading Infrastructure Systems: Numerous crypto exchange systems/bots have been formed as a result of advancements in computer science and bitcoin trading. A technique of cryptocurrency trading is called Capfolio. This method uses research platforms and specialized hardware systems. CCXT is another cryptocurrency trading system that supports a variety of cryptocurrency exchange markets, and with the help of computer technologies and bots, this system helps the investor to find the analytics data.

Real-time Cryptocurrency Trading Systems: Clients, servers, and databases make up a real-time bitcoin trading system. Traders log in to the server using a web application to purchase and sell crypto assets. The server creates a code that utilizes the Coin market API to obtain bitcoin market data. Finally, the database queries the server for balances, trades, and order book data.

Arbitrage Trading Systems: Christian pioneered cryptocurrency arbitrage trading methods. When there is a difference in the supply and demand levels in several platforms, there is a change in the price as well. The goal of arbitrage trading is to identify these alterations in price. With the help of this trading system, an individual can make profits by buying cryptocurrencies from a particular exchange platform and trading it on a different market for a higher price.

Turtle trading system: This trading technique was created in the 1970s. The main aim of the Turtle trading system is to create trading signals for breakouts. The size of assets will be adjusted by the trading system based on their volatility. The basic idea behind the turtle trading system is that breakouts should be bought, and the trade should be closed as soon as the prices start to reverse because the marketplace is highly fluctuating and has both uptrends and downtrends. If one wants to maximize the profits according to this system strategy, then the entry signal can be any time frame, but the exit signal should be significantly shorter if one wants to maximize the profits.

CHAPTER 8: DIGITAL TOKENS

If you have already made it this far into the book, then it's fair to say that now you have a working knowledge of cryptocurrencies and the associated technologies. Another important term that frequently comes up while discussing cryptocurrencies is Digital Tokens.

WHAT ARE DIGITAL TOKENS?
Digital Tokens, also known as crypto tokens or digital coins, are the tokenized representations of the digital wealth that one possesses, which can be used at any point in time, according to their convenience. Think of it this way, when you visit an arcade or a food court in a mall, most of these places do not accept cash; instead, they give you cards where you can store a certain amount of money that can be used for transactions. In essence, this is what happens with a digital token.

Digital tokens are either intrinsic or created with the help of software, and then they are assigned a value. Ether and Bitcoin are examples of intrinsic digital tokens. But digital tokens can also be backed by a physical asset; these tokens are called asset-backed tokens. These types of Digital tokens are issued as a representation of a claim on a physical commodity that is redeemable such as precious metals or legal tender.

HOW ARE DIGITAL TOKENS USEFUL?

Although digital tokens are widely popular, still not every place accepts Digital tokens as a form of payment. While some people are still hesitant about using these new forms of transactions, others are already taking the utmost benefits of it. The following are some items that can be purchased with Digital Tokens:

- **Tuition for University**: Nowadays, schools and universities have started to take payments for tuition in the form of digital tokens. One of the first universities to accept tuition fees in the form of digital tokens was a school in Cyprus.

- **Jewelry**: Jewelry is essential, especially for women. Now the process of buying jewelry has become even simpler, owing to the transaction using digital tokens. Bracelets, precious jewels, and watches can be bought using Digital Tokens. Reed Jewelers are one such jeweler that accepts Digital tokens.

- **Electronic Gadgets**: Many of the e-commerce stores that are dedicated to selling electronics, like Newegg, also accept digital tokens.

- **Charity**: Another thing that you can do with the help of Digital tokens is, make a donation.

Many Non-Government Organizations now accept donations in the form of digital tokens.

DIFFERENCE BETWEEN DIGITAL TOKENS AND COINS

There are a few key differences between digital tokens and coins. Some of the main differences are noted below:

- While a coin works similarly to a physical or traditional currency, meaning that they have a value of its own, a token serves a specific function of some kind, acting as an asset, depending upon the type of token, for example, a security token or utility token.

- Coins are generally operated in their blockchain and follow a protocol of their own, whereas tokens are known to use another coin's blockchain. Take, for example, the blockchain Ethereum. The coin used in this blockchain is Ether, but tokens like BAT also operate on this blockchain.

- Since digital coins have a value associated with them, they are generally used as a method of payment and making transactions. At the same time, tokens can not only be used for making transactions and acting as a medium of exchange but also to sign digital agreements. Some examples of these tokens would are Litecoin and REN.

DIFFERENT TYPES OF TOKENS

- *Security Tokens*

    Security tokens are the tokenized digital structure of traditional security. It may be a bond, right to ownership, or even an ownership arrangement in a company. These tokens are used to represent ownership. Financial institutions or organizations consider these security tokens as securities, which is why they are bound to their set of regulations.

- *Asset-Backed Tokens*

    When digital claims on any physical entity are backed by an asset, then they are said to be Asset-backed tokens. Any physical entity ranging from real estate, art, crude oil, gold, vegetables, or pizza can serve as an asset and can be represented as tokens. Asset-backed tokens result from an evolution that would not have been possible without Blockchain Technology. Usually, the ownership of an asset-backed token also gives one the right of ownership of the asset. The value of the asset is directly proportional to the value of the token. It means that the value of the asset-backed token depends on the worth of the assigned asset.

Asset-backed tokens have great significance as they have the potential to solve problems created due to the crisis of devalued currencies and also inflation. For new investors, asset-backed tokens also serve as an alternative to the stock market, which is highly unpredictable. Asset-backed tokens are a unique blend of the liquidity of a digital asset and the hard values of a physical asset.

- ***Transactional Tokens***

    Transactional Tokens are equivalent to traditional currencies but with additional benefits. The additional benefit mostly means the exclusion of intermediaries. This makes the transactions faster and more efficient. They are the units of accounting and are used in trading goods or for obtaining various services. Some examples of transactional tokens are the very famous Bitcoin and Dai.

- ***Utility Tokens***

    Utility tokens are those tokens that give the holder admittance to a service or a product that is based on the Blockchain. These are not created to be invested directly, but rather they serve as a means to pay for the various products and services within a specific Blockchain niche. In simpler terms, Utility Tokens are quite similar to store credit; you cannot buy anything from anywhere with store credit, but you can avail the products and services of that particular store.

On an existing protocol on the blockchain, Utility tokens are incorporated, and then they are used to access the services of that protocol. Some of the examples of Utility Tokens are Basic Attention Token or BAT, 0x (ZRX), Chainlink or LINK, Binance Coin (BNB), Aurora (AOA), Zilliqa (ZIL), etc.

TOKEN SALES

The initial phase of token offering, which happens before a cryptocurrency is ready for public use in trading, is known as a token sale. Token sales are very important for a project as their main function is to raise funds for the project to carry it forward. With the increasing numbers of tokens in the market, token sales allow the developers of a project to interest and attract potential investors in the initial stages of their project.

A good way to predict whether a project will be successful or not is to look at its token sales, which are details in the whitepapers of the projects and help in increasing the value of the tokens. Another knowledge that can be gathered by looking at a project's token sales is to what extent a project agrees to sell privately to raise sufficient funds to continue making progress.

TYPES OF TOKEN SALES

Since the role of token sales is so crucial to the development of a project and serves a part in increasing its popularity and market value, there are several kinds of token sales to choose from. Some of them are detailed below.

- **Initial Coin Offering (ICO)** - This type of token sale is ideal for companies having projects which want to generate funds by creating a novel app, coin, or service. To generate funds using ICO, a project's developers must first focus on the structure. An ICO can have different structures like Static supply and static price (where the total number of tokens, as well as their prices, is fixed) Static supply, and (where the total amount of funds received to determine the individual price of a token) Dynamic price.

- **Initial Exchange Offering (IEO)** – IEO is similar to ICO in terms of its aim, which is to raise funds for a project, but the difference between the two is that, unlike ICO, where the fundraising is carried out by the developers of the project themselves, in initial exchange offering, the fundraising is carried out by a well-known exchange's fundraising platform, for instance, Binance Launchpad. Investors can directly buy tokens using their exchange wallets, making it easier for users to carry out transactions.

- **Initial DEX Offering (IDO)** – IDO uses a decentralized exchange (DEX). It is a relatively cheaper and simpler method for projects to gather funding through the distribution of their tokens. Developers of a project are required to provide their tokens to the decentralized exchange, and the DEX carries out the final distribution of the tokens as well as the transfer, which are all automated and use smart contracts on the blockchain.

- **Security Tokens Offering (STO)** – A security token offering is a type of token sale where digital securities, which are tokenized, are sold in security token exchanges. As of 2022, there are a minimum of 30 security token offering service providers, some of which are MemePad, PathFund, AMPnet, SafeMeme, and more. Security Tokens Offering has a lot more regulations as compared to the other types of token sales because these tokens are classified as securities. The benefit of security token offerings is that it offers the same advantages one would expect from traditional securities, such as voting rights, shares, and dividends.

WHERE TO FIND THESE TYPES OF OFFERINGS AND WHAT TO KEEP IN MIND WHILE RESEARCHING THEM

To be able to find these types of offerings and participate in them, there are a few steps you need to follow.

1. **Registration on an Exchange** – First, you will need to register using a cryptocurrency exchange, for which you will need to buy a certain amount of cryptocurrency if you do not have any. After which, you will be required to complete the registration process, which may take a few days due to the KYC and AML regulations.

2. **Exchange Fiat Currency-** After you are done with the registration and have money in your cryptocurrency exchange account, you will have to exchange it for the cryptocurrency of your choice, which you will receive in your digital wallet.

3. **Transfer Coins to a Controlled Blockchain Wallet-** For safety reasons, it is advised that you move your coins from the exchange to a blockchain wallet as soon as possible.

4. **Setting up a Wallet-** You will need to have an Ethereum wallet to participate in token sales.

Remember to always back up your wallet and store the 12-word seed in a secure place.

5. **Buy Tokens**- When the token sale begins, you must transfer your ETH to the specified address, and you will receive your tokens after the sale ends, which may take a few days.

6. **Secure Your Tokens**- Remember to transfer your tokens to a more secure wallet for safety.

One of the few factors to keep in mind when dealing with token sales is that in certain cases, hackers can manipulate trade sales websites by replacing the real web address with their own, which can trick you into sending your cryptocurrency to the hacker's digital wallet instead of the genuine one. So you should always double-check the web address, payment amount, and all the details before making any deal. It is always better to analyze the risks before making a transaction.

DECENTRALIZED FINANCE (DEFI)

DeFi is the term used for the various types of projects and applications available for public use on the blockchain network, which is oriented toward the financial aspect of the blockchain. The applications under DeFi are all peer-to-peer and do not require access rights for trading financial tools. Most applications and projects are built on the Ethereum network. These applications use smart contracts, which are automated to carry out the necessary functions that are required to be performed for users to access the applications with an internet connection. DeFi is a quickly evolving technology and is free from the control that institutions and banks have on a financial system.

One of the key features of DeFi is that the transfer of funds is very quick and takes only seconds and, at most, minutes. DeFi connects people from all around the globe, irrespective of color, race, gender, pay, wealth, and geographic location. The only things a user needs to connect to DeFi are a phone or computer and an internet connection. Another important feature of DeFi is that since it is based on blockchain technology, all of its operations are available for public view, providing users with the utmost transparency.

DEFI PLATFORMS AND HOW TO USE THEM

There are multiple platforms that a user can choose from when it comes to DeFi. Following are some of the most popular DeFi platforms on the market:

- **PancakeSwap-** This platform was launched in September 2020. So far, it has over 3,3 million users worldwide, making it one of the largest used DeFi platforms. The various features enjoyed by users of this platform are trading different assets, NFTs, farm liquidity, and joining mining pools. This platform uses CAKE tokens, which are extremely expensive. It is built on the BNB chain. The benefit of using this platform is that it offers very high-speed transactions with very few transaction fees.

- **Katana-** Katana was launched in November 2021 and is still relatively new. It allows users to join mining pools, farm liquidity for rewards, swap assets, and offer other such benefits. It is also a highly popular DeFi platform and has a high user base of Axie Infinity. RON is the native asset of this platform.

- **Trader Joe-** This platform was launched in April 2021 and is developed on the Avalanche network. People using this platform can join mining pools, trade digital assets, and farm liquidity with lend assets and stake tokens. The token to the platform is called JOE.

- **SushiSwap-** This platform was launched in August 2020. Although this platform is a little controversial, it has a key advantage, which is that it supports a wide variety of blockchains such as BNB chain, Polygon, Ethereum, Avalanche, Harmony, and many more. Users are allowed to stack yields, swap or earn them, lend and even borrow them.

- **Raydium-** This platform was launched in February 2021. It provides its users the benefit of very high-speed transactions, yield farming, and shared liquidity. This platform is supercharged by Solana, and its native token is RAY.

BORROWING AND LENDING OF DEFI

By introducing the element of borrowing and lending, DeFi has brought a new light to the finance system on the blockchain network. Often known as "Open Finance." Decentralized lending has provided users who have invested in crypto opportunities to gather yields annually. At the same time, decentralized borrowing has given users the benefit of borrowing money at a definite interest rate. The aim of borrowing and lending protocols of decentralized finance or DeFi is to provide users with financial services and simultaneously ensure that the needs of the cryptocurrency market are met.

One of the most famous DeFi lending and borrowing platforms, Compound Finance, was launched in 2018. It was developed in the Ethereum blockchain, and it aims to provide users the liberty to gain interest by lending or borrowing out assets and earning high.

CHAPTER 9: MINING

So far, several important topics have been covered in the previous chapters. It is alright. If you have trouble understanding everything in one read, that's okay. Remember to take a break if you feel like you are covering too many topics at once. Cryptocurrency and blockchain technology are both very vast fields and harbor a lot of information and technicalities that one needs to be made familiar with to develop a knowledge and understanding of the topics.

During this chapter, you will learn about an aspect of cryptocurrencies called mining and staking. You will be learning about its details, how they are done, the various mining platforms available on the market, and the pros and cons of mining and staking.

WHAT IS MINING?

In simple terms, mining refers to the systematic procedure of generation and distribution of cryptocurrencies by networks of specialized computers and verification of new transactions. The cryptocurrencies that are often mined are Bitcoin or Ethereum. Mining involves the use of extensive, decentralized networks of computers from all around the globe, which verify and secure the blockchains.

This act runs in a cycle where the miners are awarded new coins by the blockchain for verifying, maintaining, and securing the transactions on the network, which acts as an incentive for the miners to continue to do so. Mining is a very competitive process, where miners compete with each other to receive coins.

HOW DOES MINING WORK?

Cryptocurrencies can be obtained by users in three ways: by using exchange platforms like Coinbase, where you can buy them with traditional currency, receive them as payments for services/goods you offer, or mine them virtually.

Mining requires the use of specialized computers. These computers carry out all the necessary calculations, which in turn help to verify and keep a record of all the new bitcoin or any other cryptocurrency transactions and ensure that the blockchain is secure. A massive amount of computing power is required to verify the blockchain during mining, which has to be provided by the miners. Generally, companies buy mining hardware and pay for the massive computing power and electricity required to perform the mining on the blockchain, in return for which they receive new coins as rewards. In general, the amount of which is higher than the amount spent on electricity spent, thereby making the transaction a profitable one.

Mining gives miners a sense of competition, as the network holds a lottery system in which every computer is in a race against each other to be the first to correctly guess the "hash." Hash is a 64-digit hexadecimal number required to be guessed by the miner's computers, and the first computer to successfully do so receives the maximum amount of coins as a reward.

The winner of this process has to update the blockchain with the newly verified transactions, hence making a new addition to the blockchain, which takes place approximately every 10 minutes. As of now, the reward for mining is approx 6.25 bitcoin. The number of bitcoins received will be halved every four years until no more bitcoins can be mined.

HOW CAN ONE MINE CRYPTOCURRENCY?

If you are interested in mining bitcoins or any other type of cryptocurrency, you may find the following information helpful. Although you must keep in mind that the power required to perform mining is very high, so it may be expensive for you to do so alone. If you have arranged the necessary power requirements, then you will be good to go and begin mining cryptocurrency.

Individual Mining – This is when a single user performs the mining using specialized miner hardware, which is a necessary requirement along with a stable and high-speed internet connection. This was more common until 2010 when individual mining was cheaper than today. But you should not lose hope, as new currencies are released in the market all the time, and you may just be lucky enough to find one which values proof-of-work (PoW) over proof-of-stake (PoS).

Cloud Mining – In this type of mining, you can invest in a cloud mining service, where you will be charged monthly to participate. Users often are comfortable taking this risk and investing in cloud mining. However, it is advised that you remember that this type of mining does not guarantee a return on investment. So if you want to try it out and participate, you must be willing to bear the loss if it does occur.

Mining Pools – In this type of mining system, different organizations come together and combine their resources to produce a large number of hardware that are specialized for mining purposes. Such pools also welcome users to join their hardware to the pool and are also open to the public. Some of these pools are formed by private individuals who group and mine coins. At the same time, these pools can be public pools, where anyone can earn cryptocurrencies in return for sharing their computing power. The rewards in such groups are divided among the participant miners depending on their contribution to the computing power. Fees are usually taken from miners participating in these pools for the smooth running of the pool.

WHAT IS STAKING?

Staking is the term used for the process by which many cryptocurrencies verify their transactions. It permits users to earn rewards on the cryptocurrencies they hold. Staking refers to committing your crypto assets to verify transactions and support the blockchain network.

A good amount of passive income can be earned by staking crypto as they offer high rates of interest for staking. In order to do that, it is necessary to know how staking works. Staking is available with cryptocurrencies that use the proof-of-stake (PoS) model to complete transactions. Proof-of-stake in cryptocurrency is a means of validating transactions. It is known for its high efficiency.

The benefit of this is that this is a more energy-efficient alternative to the traditional proof-of-work model. Proof-of-work uses mining hardware that employs computing power to make necessary mathematical calculations.

HOW IS STAKING DONE?

New transactions are added to the blockchain network via staking, in the case of cryptocurrencies that use the proof-of-stake model. As mentioned, users have to first deposit their coins to the cryptocurrency protocol, after which validators are chosen to verify and confirm transactions. The chance of a user being chosen as a validator is high if he or she has deposited a huge number of coins. New crypto coins are minted and distributed as a reward to the blockchain validator after each block is added. Oftentimes, the rewards received are the same type of coins that were staked by the user.

If you are interested in staking and are interested in trying it out, this is a good way to do so. Simply follow the steps:

Invest in a Cryptocurrency That Uses Proof-Of-Stake —Staking can only take place on cryptocurrencies that use a proof-of-stake model and not for all sorts of cryptocurrencies. So the first and foremost task that you have to perform is to research the cryptocurrencies which use the PoS model and learn about them in some detail. Some such cryptocurrencies are Ethereum (ETH), Solana (SOL), Cardano (ADA), Polkadot (DOT), etc. Try to find out the important details about the cryptocurrency that you are willing to invest in, like how they work, their staking process, and staking rewards.

Transfer The Cryptocurrency To a Digital Wallet on The Blockchain – Purchasing a cryptocurrency may take up to a few days. The crypto you purchase will be stored in the exchange where you bought it. Few exchange platforms have staking services of their own, but in case the one you have selected does not offer such programs, you will need to transfer your cryptocurrencies to a crypto wallet. Doing so will ensure more safety of your cryptocurrencies. You will have to select the option to deposit your cryptocurrency and also specify the type of crypto you will be depositing. After doing this, you will receive a wallet address that you can use to store your crypto from the exchange platform and make future transactions.

Participate In a Staking Pool – There are other methods of staking other than pool staking, but this is the preferred method by miners. You can work independently if you like, but in the case of pool mining, users can join their funds in these staking pools to stand a better chance of earning staking rewards, when you are researching for a pool, consider the size of the pool as it plays an important role. Large pools which have several users are more likely to be oversaturated and can limit the number of rewards received, whereas small pools are less likely to be selected to validate blocks. Hence, choose a medium-sized pool. Also, dig into the pool's reliability and fees before making a final decision.

CRYPTO MINING RIGS AND ELECTRICITY

The "rig" refers to a customized PC, which has all the elements that a normal computer has, such as a CPU, RAM, storage, and motherboard, but what makes it different is the graphics card, which does all the work when it comes to mining cryptocurrencies. So the main lead is taken by the GPU and not the CPU.

For mining purposes, you often need to connect several graphics cards to a single computer system. For the system to run efficiently, you will also need a motherboard that can handle multiple graphics cards and more than one power supply unit (PSU) if you want to perform heavy mining.

With the increasing number of people joining mining platforms, the chances of miners solving the hash increase dramatically. Along with that, with the accumulation of all the computer systems and electricity consumption goes very high.

Before you set up a mining rig, you should be aware of the following:

- Ensuring that all the components of the pc work perfectly well with each other. Sometimes it can be tricky as setting up a mining rig means incorporating different hardware parts into a single system and they should all be compatible with eav other.

- You will require a high amount of electricity and power to make the system run and perform mining. If not checked, it can cost you astronomically. Finding out how much power you will need and choosing the right power supply for the rig.

- Setting up a mining rig is going to be expensive, so you need to make up your mind and check your expenses before making a decision.

BEST MINING PLATFORMS

There are several mining platforms you can choose from to participate as a miner. Some of the most popular mining platforms and their key features are described below:

- **GMINERS**- This platform is a cloud service and is most suitable for beginners. It is designed for easy investments in bitcoin mining and can be operated on your PC or mobile. This platform has been described as reliable, secure, and profitable by miners. It is also compatible with several devices, so accessing the platform is not a problem for beginners. It also offers multiple payment methods, and personal managers are available for every customer.

- **SHAMINING**- This platform is equally suitable for advanced users, as well as for beginners who are mining for the very first time. The interface of this platform is quite simple and very easy to use, which makes it popular as a mining platform. There are many features offered by the platform, such as an income calculator and real-time statistics. It is also compatible with any OS and accepts different payment methods such as MasterCard, Visa, IBAN, and many more. This is the perfect choice for users who do not want to spend a lot on investments.

- **ECOS**- This platform is one of the best platforms on the market when it comes to transparency. It has over 90,000 users from all around the globe. It supports cloud mining, as well as wallet, investment portfolios, exchange, and savings. It also has a calculator feature and a wide range of contacts. ECOS offers a free mining contract for one month after registration.

- **Minedollars**- This platform is best for diversified mining and is available in more than 100 countries. This platform is highly regulated. The key features of this platform are that it provides users with a referral program, where a user is awarded a 3% commission if he or she refers the platform to a friend. It also gives its users a reward of $10 when they sign up for the first time, which can be withdrawn.

- **Pionex**- This platform is very efficient if you want to set up automatic deposits to your external wallet. Its key features include order history tracking and spot market charting. This platform also gives users the choice to decide whether they want to use manual trading or bot trading. Using this platform, a user can trade crypto with leverage of approximately four times more than the initial capital. This platform has 16 different trading bots which can automatically conduct trades if you do not wish to do it manually.

RISKS OF MINING AND STAKING

Like everything associated with crypto, mining and staking have their advantages as well as disadvantages. Some of the risks of mining and staking crypto are given below:

- Crypto is highly volatile, which means that its prices keep fluctuating and can drop at any given moment. If you have staked assets and they suffer a sudden drop in value, it causes you to be distressed and may outweigh any interest that you earn from them.

- The process of unstaking crypto takes a long time, sometimes more than a week.

- If you want to stake your coins, it may require you to keep them locked for a certain period, during which you will not be able to do any transactions with them.

REWARDS OF MINING AND STAKING

Mining and staking bring a set of rewards for users to enjoy too. Some of the benefits associated with them are:

- By mining and staking, you will be contributing to maintaining the security of the blockchain as well as its efficiency.

- Staking gives users the benefit of earning more crypto with high-interest rates.

- Staking is a convenient way to earn coins and interest from cryptocurrency holdings.

CHAPTER 10: NFT

If I have to describe it in the simplest terms, NFT is a non-interchangeable unit of data that is unique in nature and is stored on the blockchain. The respective owner of the NFT gets proof of that ownership certificate given to him by the digital ledger. Nevertheless, there are still a few people out there who have no clue how Non-Fungible Tokens have shaken up the entire world in such a drastic way. Non-Fungible Tokens can be generally associated with digital art, however, there are many different types of NFTs. They have proven to be the latest trend these days. They boomed in 2021, and since then, everyone has been going crazy about them in the crypto world.

The power of NFTs lies in the fact that it is equally associated with both virtual and digital assets. At the same time, due to the recent advancement in technology, many modern applications of non-fungible tokens have been created. It has been done with the intention of making NFT transactions more secure and transparent.

DIFFERENT TYPES OF NFT AND HOW IT WORKS

As I have already mentioned, there are different kinds of NFTs in the market, and a few of them are: Artworks, Sports Memorabilia, Virtual Land, Domain Names, Ticketing, NFT fashion, Miscellaneous Online items, identity, real-world assets, music, memes, video-games assets, and collectibles.

- **Artworks** – Artworks are an extremely popular category of NFTs. There are a large number of digital artworks that come with absolute authenticity and ownership that is issued by the digital ledger that stores these artworks.

- **Sports Memorabilia** – As you can already guess, sports collectibles represent a category that is among the most popular NFTs, and one that generally includes all the famous and memorable video clips of sports moments.

- **Virtual Land** – I am sure you have come across those games that let you acquire land in them. Yes, in NFTs, virtual lands consist of areas in the metaverse and video games. You can buy land in the metaverse with a few easy steps. Mind you, virtual land has great potential and can be used for placing advertisements. You can also create that space for virtual assets.

- **Domain Names** — By domain names, I mean the crypto domains that are minted on a blockchain. Be it Ethereum or Binance Smart Chain. The thing about crypto domains is that they do not depend on any kind of centralized authority, and that is the reason they are bought after. Another thing about domain names, they can be used to link other crypto-wallets.

WHAT ARE HIGH-VALUE NFTS?

In 2021 the world saw the NFT market explode with almost 25 billion dollars worth of trade. Here are a few of the most high-priced NFT sales to date:

- The artwork "*EVERYDAYS": THE FIRST 5000 DAYS* holds the top position. It was created by the artist Mike "Beeple" Winkelmann, and was sold at Christie's for 69.3 million dollars. Yes, you read that right. It was the first time Christie's sold an artwork purely digitally. This piece is a collage of the artist's 5000 earlier works that give the viewer an idea about his work.

- Now let's talk about the Nft which is known as the "*Clock.*" Artist Pak created this NFT, and he is known for using novel token models to fuel his projects. It was sold for 52.7 million dollars, and Pak donated the entire amount to a project that is known as the Wau Holland Stiftung Moral Courage Project.

- Remember Mike "Beeple" Winkelmann from above? Right, well, he has another spot in the top three. It was in late 2021 that he came out with another massive creation of his. Known as the *HUMAN ONE*, it is a sculpture that has digital screens on the sides, which show a person wearing a spacesuit walking through a constantly changing environment. It was sold for 28.9 million dollars.

- Next in line is *CryptoPunk#5822*. It was sold for 23.7 million dollars in February 2022. These alienated pixelated faces are extremely famous, and on top of that, this particular one is very rare.

HOW TO BUY AND SELL NFT

First things first, NFTs are bought with cryptocurrencies, and the majority of the transactions are done on *OpenSea which* is the leading marketplace for NFT transactions. Along with Ethereum, a cryptocurrency wallet will be needed for you to take part in the transaction.

Additionally, there are a few good options for Nft marketplaces like Nifty Gateway, SuperRare, etc. if you are looking for cryptocurrency wallets, two best options are MetaMask and Coinbase Wallet.

For you to start, go to the OpenSea **login page** and then connect your crypto wallet. Next, visit your profile, where you can see the collection of NFTs posted by the members; you can keep track of all your favorite marketplace activities here. At this point, you are prepared to browse through and make a potential purchase. There will be certain listings that will show a **Buy Now** option. When you go there, you can make your desired bit and also state an expiration date. When your transaction is completed, the NFT will be transferred to your wallet. There is a **Collected** tab on every profile. Your transactions will be listed there. As for OpenSea, they take 2.5 % of every transaction made through them.

If you decide to sell an existing NFT on the market, here are the easy steps to follow. First, go to your profile and then select the desired NFT that you want to sell. You will notice that towards the top right of the screen, there will be a blue **Sell** button available. Click on that and then pick the **Fixed Price** option if there is a fixed amount in your mind. You can also choose **Timed Auction** if you want people to bid on your NFT.

As far as OpenSea is concerned, they charge an account initialization fee when you first list something. In Ethereum, which is known as a "gas fee." Every seller has to pay this gas fee whenever they post an offer.

BEST PLATFORMS FOR NFT

Your transaction becomes easier when you choose the right marketplace. It is therefore crucial that you choose the right marketplace. It could be confusing given there is a wide range of marketplaces to consider from. Below I am listing five of the best beginner-friendly NFT marketplaces:

- **NFT LaunchPad** – A relatively newer marketplace, NFT LaunchPad has already carved its niche. It has been designed by creators while keeping all the possible needs of other creators in mind. You can easily mint your own NFTs here using the MP4 format. That is the reason it is such a hit among beginners. The USP of NFT Launchpad is how easy it is to use. It collaborates with Polygon and Binance Smart Chain. It is very easy to do all your transactions with MetaMask wallets here.

- **Crypto.com** – Another fast-growing NFT marketplace is Crypto.com which has a lot to provide to both collectors and creators. Why is this becoming a favorite of many? That is because crypto.com offers some of the lowest fees you can get on buying and selling. It has very recently launched an integration with the Ethereum blockchain, and that is why you can come across thousands of NFTs on this platform.

- **Binance** – Binance can be considered the largest crypto exchange platform. Founded in 2017 by Changpeng Zhao, it was initially based in China. That is why Binance has a lot of advantages over any other crypto exchanging platform, be it for purchasing or selling. Because the Binance network is intrinsically embedded in the NFT market, funding any purchase or swapping tokens becomes really easy. It is not necessary for you to choose which NFTs you would like to buy on Binance, in fact, to make things interesting, Binance marketplace offers you "mystery boxes," which are basically a collection of a handful of NFTs at a flat and low price.

Binance makes sure to offer you a massive collection of cryptos along with new coins being listed continuously. This will ensure you have a smooth trading experience. When using Binance, you can enjoy a wide range of leverage and high liquidity to perform any trade. As a user of Binance, you will be protected 24/7 as there are multiple security features for you, including 300 million dollars worth of insurance, ensuring your safety.

- **OpenSea** – If your aim is to look for massive diversity in NFTs or probably to go and look for expensive and rare NFTs that are up for sale, OpenSea is the place for you. At this moment, OpenSea is the largest marketplace for rare and expensive NFTs in the entire world. One of the biggest USPs of OpenSea is that they support almost 150 different cryptocurrencies for payment. What that means is you will save money as well as time if you go to compare it with any other marketplace, where they force you to exchange your tokens before you make any purchase.

- **Rarible** – Rarible is undoubtedly the best place if you are looking for first-time NFT creators. Considered one of the top markets for discovery, you can very easily browse through the most trending of all the collections, look for top sellers, and at the same time ongoing auctions in Rarible. Compared to other marketplaces, the layout of this platform is much more inviting. The prices on Rarible are denominated in Ethereum, and at the same time, you can use tokens of the respective platform to make your purchases. Rarible charges you around a 2.5% transaction fee.

RISK REGARDING NFT

Given that NFTs are helping digital creators make a lot of money, it, unfortunately, comes with the risk of considerable online fraud. When you are thinking of getting into an NFT transaction, I would suggest that you consider all the risks present and then make a decision. Being aware of the risks will help you get a better idea of what precautions to take. A few of the risks are –

- **Challenges Regarding Evaluation** – One of the most prominent problems faced is that of setting the price for the particular NFT. All the factors on which the price can depend are subjective, namely uniqueness, creativity, owners, etc. So quite naturally, fluctuations are an unavoidable part of setting the price. It is not possible for people to locate the driving factors of the NFTs. Mainly due to this reason, the prices going up and down is a very common factor in all NFT markets.

- **Cyber Treats** – The popularity of anything will give rise to fraud and replication of the same. NFT is no different. One can find plenty of duplicates of the NFT stores on the internet. They are made to look authentic by the logo and also the content. Fake NFT stores can very well counterfeit their sales. It could also happen that some fake artists might try and impersonate the works of other famous artists and try to sell those. Many people are successfully scammed by these fake NFTs.

- **Legal Challenges** – At present, there is no international body governing Non-Fungible Tokens, and naturally, there are no strict or fixed laws, regulations, or any legalization procedure for that matter. Although different countries are moving ahead with their respective legal approaches, it is not having the desired impact.

- **Intellectual Property Rights** – A very important topic to bring under consideration is the ownership of any non-fungible token. It falls under your duty to see whether the NFT that you are purchasing falls under the ownership of the seller or not. You need to do this because many times, a seller might pose as the original owner while the actual scenario might be the exact opposite. It could well be a replica. In that case, you only have the right to use the NFT. For that, what needs to be done is to look into the metadata that the smart contract has. All details of ownership are mentioned there. There is a rule that if the seller is not the owner, they can only display their NFTs and not sell them.

- **Making NFTs and Securities Synonymous** – A lot of people treat the act of purchasing NFTs like a mode of collecting securities. Even the chairman of SEC said that the majority of the NFTs in the market at present are being bought and sold as a medium of security. The scenario is different, however. The supreme court has related NFT transactions with investment contracts. If at all NFTs were to pass as a form of security, it definitely needs to go through a test for them to attain credibility.

- **Smart Contract Risks** – One of the most prominent problems raging in the Non-Fungible Token market currently is smart contract risks and NFT maintenance. There have been many cases where frauds and hackers have posed an attack on a decentralized finance network (Defi), and they have stolen a large amount of crypto. In recent times, a mentionable attack was made on Poly Network, which is a renowned DeFi protocol. Hackers have stolen NFT worth 600 million dollars. The main reason behind this theft was inadequate smart contract security. The flaws that existed on the smart contract platform were successfully exploited by hackers. In case you didn't know, the Poly network is extremely useful when swapping tokens on different blockchains. What does this tell us? This tells us that no matter how strong the platform is, even a tiny flaw can be taken advantage of and exploited.

CONCLUSION

Now that you have reached the last part of the book. I hope the book was informative and answered all your questions.

Bitcoin has become a household name and is often used synonymously for digital assets. Bitcoin was the first kind of cryptocurrency that was launched in 2009. You probably see a lot of people investing in Bitcoins, and that motivates you to walk down that path to see how rewarding these investments can be. But before you dive into this market, it is important that you have your basic knowledge up to date. Using an example, let us brush up on the concept of cryptocurrency once again.

Say you have a basketball and you give it to your friend. Your friend now receives the ball physically, which means that the transaction took place from one person to another, and no one else has been a witness to this exchange. Now, your friend has one basketball, and you have none, and because you have given it to your friend, you have no control over it any longer. Now think of this basketball to be in a digital form. You send it to your friend again, but this time it is a digital ball. Since the transaction was not person-to-person(i.e. physically), there is no way you can know if the basketball has been transferred in its original form. Multiple copies can be made of the ball and can be sent to many other friends.

Here is where the term 'ledger' comes into the picture, and it is important to understand how it is used. What is a ledger? A ledger is a database responsible for keeping track of all the transactions that happen to and from these accounts. You may think of it as a directory that keeps a record of the transactions that are received or transferred from these accounts. Coming back to the basketball scenario, the ledger will be the third party that will ensure that your friend gets what you send them in its original form and prevents any kind of alteration/duplication. In the case of banks, there is only one centralized ledger that only the bank can access but in the crypto world each and every investor has their own ledger where they can trace all the transactions that have taken place.

After understanding the concept and working of these assets, you would be further inclined to find out how you can transact the money in the crypto market and where your money actually goes. This will bring us to the concept of crypto wallets. Remember what they are? If not, do not worry; let me tell you again. Most of us have a bank account where we store our money, but this account of ours is controlled by the bank authorities. If you are a user who wishes to trade in cryptocurrencies, you will need a wallet too, which is known as a crypto wallet or a digital wallet that, unlike your bank account, will be in your control. These digital wallets will help you to store and transact digital currencies. These wallets are where you will organize your crypto portfolio. Crypto wallets are applications that allow crypto users to store and retrieve their digital assets.

There are two addresses in these wallets – a private address and a public address. What function does the public address have? It is the place where you send the cryptocurrency. If you wish to send cryptocurrency to another person's wallet, you will need their public address. You will need to feed in their public address and send the cryptocurrency to that address. You need the private key when you want to access the assets that you have received. You may think of the private key as your password for the wallet transactions.

There are several kinds of wallets that are available. Wallets that can be accessed through mobile apps are called hot wallets, and there are external physical wallets too that look like USB sticks. Setting up a crypto wallet and knowing how to use it is a must before you trade your first currency. If you want to get started using your own wallet, check out chapter 3 again, where everything about wallets has been discussed in detail, from what they are, their function, how they work, the various kinds that are available, to how you need to set them up.

Crypto wallets are central to crypto transactions and provide asset security, which is why you should wisely choose one for yourself. Let me remind you of the important criteria you should consider when selecting a crypto wallet.

To begin with, the kind of crypto wallet you choose will depend on your needs and the experience you have as a crypto trader. But, wherever you locate yourself at the experience level, you must always first consider the wallet's security. Secondly, the transaction fees vary from app to app. Some apps allow you to customize each transaction fee which is good for reducing your transaction costs. Next, you would want to find out if your wallet allows the transaction of the currency you want to trade, as not all wallets support all kinds of cryptocurrencies. Finally, look for a wallet that offers customer support round the clock as a part of their customer service. Just as mindful as you would be with your banking service, you would need to check crypto wallets too carefully before putting your trust and assets in them.

You must be thinking why I am constantly harping on the security factor even though we all know how risky crypto trading is. This is because the risk factors associated with crypto transactions should not stop you from exploring what is deemed as the 'future of finance.' To trade in digital assets, you must acquire an appetite for risk. Does that mean you are bound to incur losses with every transaction you make? Not really, but it may happen at some point in your crypto career. However, it is possible to manage these risks if not completely eradicate them, and in this book, a chapter has been dedicated solely to ways you can combat these risks. The chapter mentions everything from what risks could come your way when dealing with crypto assets, how you can measure these risks and prevent them from claiming your hard-earned money, ways in which these risks can be avoided, and also some of the important things you must watch out while trading digital coins.

Here, while talking about risks, I would like to remind you of some common mistakes that you must avoid at all costs. Firstly, never buy a coin or a token just because the prices are low. Low prices always do not represent bargains. You need to watch out here. Stop and look for the reason the prices could be low. Secondly, refrain from going all in. The platform you are trading in may suggest that you maximize your returns by betting as much as you can, but it is healthy to invest not more than five percent of your investing capital. Thirdly, never make the mistake of thinking crypto is easy money. Beware of fraudulent intentions if anyone is trying to make you believe that. Finally, the most common mistake users make is falling for scams. To survive and do well in this ecosystem, you will need to be smart and dodge the malicious intentions of several scammers who are everywhere on this platform.

To start trading, the next important thing you would need is a crypto portfolio which simply is a collection of coins that a crypto investor or trader owns. The essential requirements for building a crypto portfolio have already been discussed thoroughly. Follow them and make your own portfolio to start trading. Building a portfolio is not where your job ends; to safeguard yourself from unplanned risks, you must also rebalance your portfolio—have you forgotten how to do that? You can always go back to the chapter on portfolio analysis and look up the step-by-step guide to ease your job.

As promised, I have tried to cover everything that would help you get started in your crypto journey, from the basic concept of it, the components you need to set up to start trading, the risks of the market, and also where you can start trading. In addition, I have attempted my best in giving out some very valuable tips on trading, value investing, and asset allocation that will give you a little more knowledge about assets and currencies and will put you ahead of others who are starting with a very preliminary knowledge. The one thing that I would want you to specifically take away from this book is the tricks of trading in this industry with a minimum risk. Hopefully, through the chapters, all your basic queries about the crypto space have been answered and have prepared you to take on the crypto world.

This is an era of information, and everything you would need to know to navigate your way through the crypto world can be found in several blogs, websites, and other books. But, that you have chosen this book over the plenty of others available makes me want to express my gratitude from the bottom of my heart. Thank you for placing your trust in me and letting me be your guide in this journey of yours. I am beyond grateful that you have given my book your valuable time, and I would hope that I have been able to deliver on the promise I made at the beginning of the book and on your expectations. We all have had some scope to focus on new things with the pandemic, and

I am assuming you are here reading this because you, too, wanted to give crypto investment a shot. These are challenging times, so I hope you and your family are taking good care of themselves. Over everything, I would want my beloved readers to stay healthy.

If you liked this book and if it served your purpose, do leave your honest review on Amazon. I consider you, my readers, to be my best critics, so I will eagerly wait for your response. I write with utmost honesty, seeing that I cater to what you want to read, and I would hope for the same transparency from you in the form of your valuable reviews. It is your reviews that help me grow as an author. Looking forward to your reviews and meeting you next time through another topic in another book, and wishing you the best in your crypto journey. May you have a fun and safe time, and may your fortunes grow abundantly.

Shawn Colon

ABOUT THE AUTHOR

Shawn Colon is a US-based writer. He is passionate about helping beginners make a living from their artistic talent. He believes in the principles of Philosophy and that people should live their dreams and not get sucked into a life of doing something they don't like. He is a teacher, investor, gamer, and coffee nerd who loves to meditate and keep things sane in this overthinking world.

Printed in Great Britain
by Amazon